Europe and the Superpower Balance

by A. W. DePorte

CONTENTS

	Foreword, *by Stanley Hoffmann*	3
1	Europe: Death of a State System	5
2	Indian Summer of Europe: 1918–1940	13
3	World War II: From One System to Another	20
4	Entrance of the Superpowers	25
5	The Cold War Begins	33
6	The Building of a New State System	39
7	Consolidation of the Two-Bloc System: The German Problem	47
8	Challenges: East and West	54
9	Challenges: Within the West	61
10	Toward the Future	75
	Talking It Over	77

HEADLINE Series 247, December 1979 $1.40

Cover by Design Works

The Author

A. W. DePORTE is a career official of the U.S. Department of State, currently serving as director of the Western European office of the Bureau of Intelligence and Research. He holds a doctorate in international relations from the University of Chicago and is the author of *De Gaulle's Foreign Policy, 1944-1946* (Cambridge, Harvard University Press, 1968). The views expressed in this publication are his own and do not necessarily reflect the policies or the views of the Department of State or of the Council on Foreign Relations.

The Foreign Policy Association

The Foreign Policy Association is a private, nonprofit, nonpartisan educational organization. Its purpose is to stimulate wider interest and more effective participation in, and greater understanding of, world affairs among American citizens. Among its activities is the continuous publication, dating from 1935, of the HEADLINE Series pamphlets. The authors of these pamphlets are responsible for factual accuracy and for the views expressed. FPA itself takes no position on issues of United States foreign policy.

Editorial Advisory Committee

Hans J. Morgenthau, *chairman*
W. Phillips Davison
John Lewis Gaddis
Keith Goldhammer
Antonie T. Knoppers

William H. McNeill
Edwin Newman
Stanley E. Spangler
Joan E. Spero
Richard H. Ullman

The HEADLINE Series (ISSN 0017-8780) is published February, April, August, October and December by the Foreign Policy Association, Inc., 205 Lexington Ave., New York, N.Y. 10016. Chairman, Carter L. Burgess; Editor, Wallace Irwin, Jr.; Associate Editor, Gwen Crowe. Subscription rates, $7.00 for 5 issues; $13.00 for 10 issues; $18.00 for 15 issues. Single copy price $1.40. Discount 25% on 10 to 99 copies; 30% on 100 to 499; 35% on 500 to 999; 40% on 1,000 or more. Payment must accompany order for $5 or less. Second-class postage paid at New York, N.Y. Copyright 1979 by Foreign Policy Association, Inc. Composed and printed at Science Press, Ephrata, Penn.

Library of Congress Catalog No. 79-92257
ISBN 0-87124-058-0

Foreword
by Stanley Hoffmann

If I had to give a prize to the most sensible book written about the role of Western Europe in the postwar international system, A. W. DePorte's would be the winner. It manages to be both important and original. It is important because of its thesis: to quote General de Gaulle (whose challenge to the postwar order DePorte analyzes with great finesse), the German problem *is* the European problem—ever since Bismarck unified, in the heart of the Continent, a nation too strong to be contained by traditional balance-of-power politics. Germany's might launched two world wars. The only solution to the German problem, *i.e.* the only way of containing German dynamism, has been the partition of Germany and of Europe, which the superpowers achieved—not quite deliberately—after the end of World War II. Precisely because this partition has served the interests of both superpowers as well as of Germany's neighbors, and because West Germany's leaders have wisely chosen to put integration with the West above the mirage of reunification, the division of the Continent has resisted all challenges.

The originality of DePorte's study lies in the startling implication of his thesis. Not only is Europe bound to remain divided, but this division is preferable—for the West Europeans at least—to any theoretical alternative, and their best efforts ought to remain at adaptation, not radical change. The stability of the East-West balance in Europe is not any more "delicate" than the balance of terror: despite shifts in this balance and in strategic doctrines, the American nuclear guarantee remains the foundation of West European security, however hard Americans

---

Stanley Hoffmann is professor of government and chairman of the Center for European Studies at Harvard University. His books include *Primacy or World Order* and other works on international affairs and U.S. foreign policy.

themselves, perversely and periodically, deny its credibility. As a result, West European integration is likely to remain a glass half-full, since many of the functions a full-fledged federal power normally carries out are actually either beyond Western Europe's reach, or accomplished in Atlantic rather than West European frameworks.

Many of these statements either contradict current clichés, or undercut recurrent fears, or deflate noble hopes. But DePorte's analyses are eminently sound. They explain why, indeed, the U.S.-West European relationship has survived all the crises which clashes of interests, the West Europeans' dependence on American security guarantees, economic interdependence and political misperceptions make both unavoidable and predictable. They also explain why the iron curtain has proved more durable than the Gaullist attempt to reunite Europe "from the Atlantic to the Urals," or East European attempts at emancipation. I know of no account of European diplomatic history from the days of Bismarck to Hitler's *Götterdämmerung* that goes to the heart of the problem more effectively than DePorte's short one, and certainly none of the innumerable studies of the cold war discusses American and Soviet policies more reasonably and persuasively than DePorte's brief but pungent analysis. He has brought to this book both his experience as a diplomat and his rigorous training as a historian. It is a rare and perfect blend. It is also a triumph of common sense over myths and hysterias, over the nostalgia for "might have been" or paranoia. It deserves not only the readers' full attention, but their gratitude.

1

Europe: Death of a State System

The first order of business for any state is to ensure its own survival. Whole systems of states have disappeared from history; but in other systems the contact and conflict among the member states—their international relations—led not to the disappearance but to the survival of most of them over long periods.

The modern European state system was (for it no longer exists) of this type. The similarities between the gross outlines of the map of Western and Central Europe of 1500 and that of today are striking. Most of the member states survived all fluctuations of power, rank and frontiers for 500 years or more. As all things changed, the states themselves persisted, along with the fundamental structure of the relations among them that made their survival possible.

> *Editor's note: This essay is an abbreviated version of Mr. DePorte's* Europe Between the Superpowers: The Enduring Balance, *a Council on Foreign Relations Book published in April 1979 by Yale University Press (Copyright © 1979 by Yale University). This adaptation from the 256-page original was made with the cooperation of the author and is printed with the permission of the copyright owner.*

We take for granted this truly extraordinary phenomenon—so much so that the final breakdown of the European state system in World War II is still often thought to be no more than a temporary departure from a millennial normalcy. In fact, the radically new situation of postwar Europe can be seen as it is only if the brute fact of the death of the prewar state system is analytically—and emotionally—grasped.

It is worth considering why the fundamental stability of the defunct European state system ensured the survival of the member states over so long a period and why it finally collapsed. For postwar Europe emerged from the prewar state system, and the long success and the circumstances of the recent death of the old system strongly color what has happened since 1945.

In the European system up to 1914, no one state, or even a group of states, could gain lasting ascendancy. The system worked in part because of almost mechanical forces. If any state seemed to be getting overly powerful and ambitious in proportion to the others, the others sooner or later leagued together to set limits to the threat (though often creating a new one, which then set the process in motion again). In part, the system also worked because, after a time, the participating states came to believe that it would, so that their ambitions and calculations were adjusted accordingly. Going further, a kind of international ethic of self-restraint grew up in the 18th and 19th centuries which condemned any drive to European hegemony, or any threat to the very existence of an established state.

The main characteristics of the old system are worth noting as points of contrast with the system which succeeded it in the mid-20th century. First, the old system was very fluid. The large states formed and reformed their groupings; the smaller ones changed protectors. Second, the system was much more colored by ideological considerations than is often thought. The political rivalries of the 16th and 17th centuries were strongly affected by religious controversy. The 19th century was full of ideology, and not only during the revolutionary and Napoleonic wars. Imperial Russia set great store during much of the century on defending conservatism; the role of France, at least up to 1870, was similarly colored, in the opposite direction.

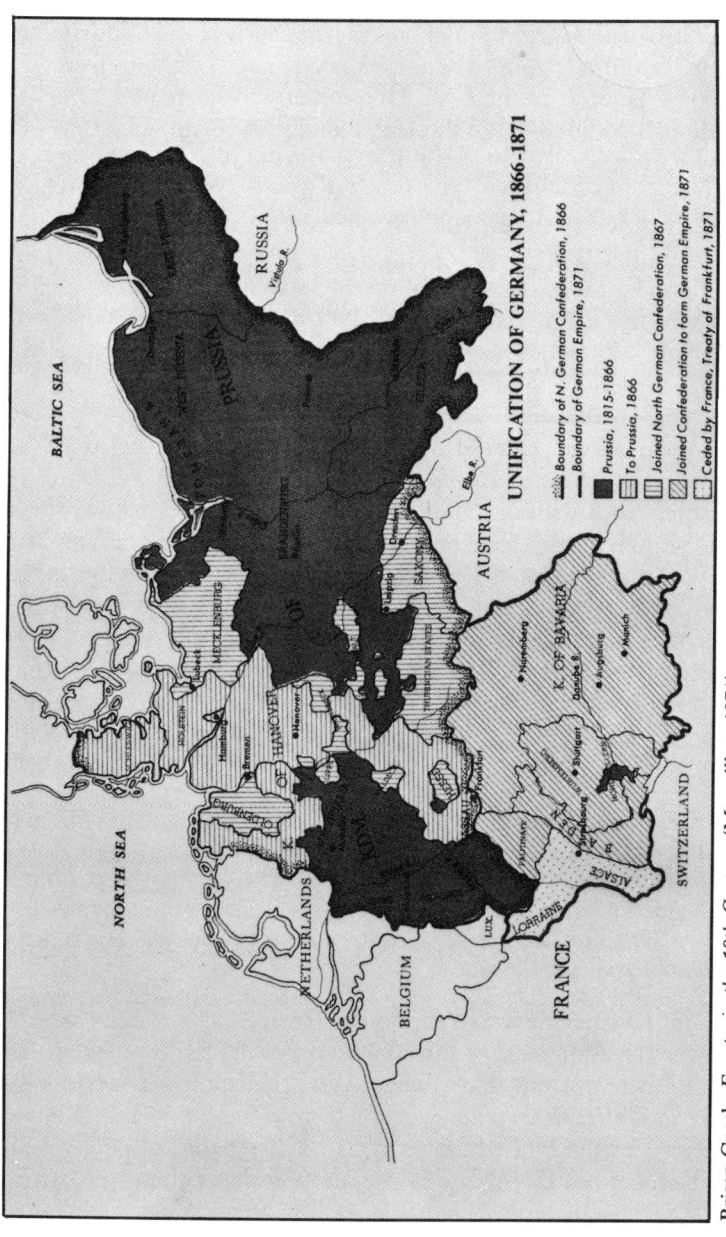

Brison Gooch, *Europe in the 18th Century* (Macmillan, 1971)

Third, the distribution of power frequently shifted. During the 16th century, Spain, France, Austria and England were the leading powers. In the 17th, Holland and Sweden joined the list, although both fell out in the 18th along with Spain, while Prussia and Russia were then added. Before the industrial revolution, the European system, characterized by five great powers amidst a crowd of lesser states, was firmly fixed in the pattern it would hold until 1918.

Fourth, the *absolute* amount of power at the command of practically all governments in 1900 was greater than those of 1800 or 1700 enjoyed, but at any given time the positions of the great powers of the day relative to each other tended to be—or become—stable.

When Russia entered the European system in the mid-18th century, it of course struck people's imagination by reason of its vastness. But with its small population, economic backwardness, and administrative weakness, Russia did not at first have any real impact on the *scale* of European politics; it entered the system as one great power among others. Still, Russian troops occupied Berlin as early as 1760, fought in northern Italy in the 1790s, and in 1814 entered Paris. After 1815, a number of people began to see Russia as something more than one great power among others. The most familiar of these prophets was Alexis de Tocqueville, who wrote in the 1830s:

> There are now two great nations in the world which, starting from different points, seem to be advancing toward the same goal: the Russians and the Anglo-Americans.... Their point of departure is different and their paths diverse; nevertheless, each seems called by some secret design of Providence one day to hold in its hands the destinies of half the world.

De Tocqueville was right in foreseeing both a new scale of power for 20th-century international politics and the states that would benefit from that change. What he could not see was the way in which the bipolar world was to come into being. Neither Russia nor the United States initiated the change of power scale in Europe, but Germany. It was not Germany, however, which was to benefit from that change, but Russia and the United

States. Telescoped in those two sentences are the decline and fall of the European system I have described and the emergence, since 1945, of a wholly different kind of system which is no mere transition to a restoration of the old order, now irrevocably gone, but a firmly established and probably long-lived successor to it.

The Transformation Begins: 1895-1914

The period 1895-1905 marked the beginning of a transformation of the international power system. Soon after 1900, for example, Britain entered into alliance with one non-European power, Japan, and began to forge a "special relationship" with another, the United States. The convergence of power rivalries on the Far East in the 1890s pointed to the development of a truly *world* power structure, still centered in Europe but no longer confined to it.

This geographic expansion was closely related to the transformation of the scale of power then under way in Europe. The pacesetter after 1870 was the newly unified German Empire. After the success of the Prussian military system in the wars of 1866 and 1870, all the European states except Britain shifted over from small professional armies to the principle of universal service. Mass armies put new importance on population; modern weapons—especially navies—on industry; both, on economic power and each country's ability to pay for these things. Some advanced rapidly toward a wholly new scale of power; others lagged farther and farther behind. (See chart on page 10.)

The most conspicuous factor overall was the rise of German military power. In modern industry, also, Germany was setting a new standard for power in Europe. But it was as overshadowed in industry by the United States (which in 1913 produced 32 million tons of steel) as in population by Russia. Thus, someone who in 1914, for example, tried to conjure up the contours of the entire political landscape for the half century before and after could not but notice the decline of Austria-Hungary and France, the growing eclipse not only of them but of Britain by Germany, and the prospect that Russia and the United States might both, in a more or less foreseeable future, overshadow even German power.

INDICES OF CHANGING POWER: HOW GERMANY AND RUSSIA TOOK THE LEAD

		Austria-Hungary	Germany	France	United Kingdom	Russia	Italy
1880	Population (millions)	37	43	37	35	93	28
	Steel production (million tons)	0.1	0.7	0.4	1.3	0	0
Eve of World War I[1]	Population (millions)	52	65	39	45	171	37
	Steel production (million tons)	2.6	17.6	4.7	7.8	4.8	0.9
Eve of World War II[2]	Population (millions)	*	70	41	47	196	43
	Steel production (million tons)	*	22.7	6.2	10.6	18.1	2.3

Sources: A.W. DePorte, *Europe Between the Superpowers*, p. 12, 13, 30; for pre-World War II population figures, United Nations *Demographic Yearbook 1958* and articles on "Germany" in *Encyclopaedia Britannica*, 1949 edition.
[1] Figures are for 1914, steel production figures for 1913.
[2] Steel production figures are for 1938. Population figures are for 1937 except those for Russia (= Soviet Union, 1940) and Germany (1939). The latter excludes 10 million Austrians and Sudeten Germans then incorporated in Hitler's "Greater Germany."
*Ceased to exist as a unit after World War I.

In 1871 the German Empire emerged as the strongest military power after its victories over Austria and France. Its success was seen at the time as modifying but not upsetting the traditional balance-of-power system. This view was due primarily to the circumspect policy of Germany under the rule of Bismarck. The

Otto von Bismarck, architect of German unification and first chancellor (1871-90) of the German Empire

Culver Pictures, Inc.

main thrust of his policy was to keep Europe quiet, the *status quo* intact, frontiers unchanged. However, those who succeeded him after 1890 found his foreign policies too narrow for the resources Germany's new industrial power placed at their command. Germany's belated efforts to make its weight felt in Europe came at a time when xenophobic popular nationalism was moving toward its disastrous climax. The disturbance created by Germany in the international atmosphere was thus intense.

Diplomatic realignments began which resulted in 1904 in the Entente Cordiale between Britain and France, and in 1907 in the formation of the Triple Entente between those two powers and Russia. Defense expenditures shot up and a period of almost permanent tension set in about 1905, during which a succession of crises threatening war accustomed many to think that a final test of arms between the two camps was inevitable.

Meanwhile, Germany's one reliable ally, Austria-Hungary, was visibly sliding down the power scale. The Austrian government decided in July 1914 that offense was the best defense and resolved to crush Serbia, once the murder of Archduke Franz Ferdinand supplied the pretext. The Germans saw no reason to abandon their one ally, with whose survival they had gratuitously and imprudently entangled themselves. Neither Germany nor Austria-Hungary sought war with Russia, Serbia's Slavic patron, or a general European war, but both were conscious of the risk and willing to take it.

Behind the specific details of the events of July 1914, most of the participants seem to have been aware of the wider crisis which their international system was undergoing. In fact, the war itself confirmed that the balance of power on which the European state system was based had already been upset and could no longer fulfill its most fundamental purpose: to guarantee the survival and the status as great powers of the principal member states.

In this sense, World War I, which revealed and precipitated a long-growing transformation, was by far the most fundamental event of the 20th century. Europe has been adapting to its consequences ever since.

The entrance of the United States into the war in 1917 suddenly transformed a European war into a world war and prevented a German victory. Britain, France, and Bolshevik Russia were thus saved from subordination to Germany. But the old self-contained European state system was not saved, for its member states had been unable to defend themselves against the power of one of them. The independence of the European states was maintained only because, as British Prime Minister George Canning had said in 1826, the New World had been called into existence to redress the balance of the Old.

2

Indian Summer of Europe: 1918-1940

The length and intensity of World War I had the effect of escalating war aims on all sides. Each government tried to justify the war to its own people not only by claiming to be defending a beleaguered fatherland against wanton aggression but also by holding out the hope that victory would produce a better international system. The allies, however, found it difficult to explain how the victory to be won at such cost would permanently ensure their security in the face of Germany's obvious power.

Their eventual solution came from President Woodrow Wilson's statement of war aims, set forth in his Fourteen Points on January 8, 1918. Confronted by the call of the new Bolshevik government in Russia for a democratic peace based on self-determination, Wilson and many others realized that the allies too had to show that they were fighting for principles. The other Allied governments were far from sharing all of Wilson's views, but they desperately needed the United States at that moment. The allies thus undertook to eliminate not only the German militarist regime but also the broader evils of the balance-of-power system, secret diplomacy, and the denial of self-determination to subject peoples.

President Wilson toured the western states in 1919, campaigning for the League of Nations. Photo shows him passing the San Francisco city hall.

However, the tide reversed itself once the war had ended and flowed strongly toward conservatives who favored a severe peace with Germany—and, hardly less important, severe measures to deal with Bolshevism in Russia. This swing was no less pronounced in the United States than in Britain, France and Italy, where "hanging the Kaiser" was the order of the day. Wilsonian principles retained supporters everywhere, but they proved frail barriers to national demands in each country.

But though revanchism in Germany may have been exacerbated by particular provisions of the Treaty of Versailles, it was, in fact, created by the defeat itself. The German army, with the homeland still uninvaded, allowed the new republic to shoulder blame for accepting a defeat which the army knew it could not prevent. The Weimar Republic had a great burden to carry as the signer of the Versailles Treaty, but an even greater one as the receiver in bankruptcy of a military defeat that the country did not accept as such.

Meanwhile, the distinctive American contribution to the settlement, the League of Nations, which should have appealed to American moralism and messianism, led Wilson's own country to reject the treaty because its opponents claimed that League membership involved an indefinite commitment to defend the peace settlement. Wilson's failure—or, rather, America's—left the European settlement standing on one leg. Britain and France had won the war only with American help, and neither their victory nor the peace settlement made them powerful enough to outweigh even the Germany of the peace settlement.

Germany was, of course, diminished and hobbled by the settlement. There were the loss of Alsace-Lorraine to France and of territory in the east to Poland; the loss of all colonies; heavy reparations; Allied occupation and permanent demilitarization of the left bank of the Rhine; and severe limitations on the size and equipment of the armed forces. But it was doubtful from the start whether the allies would preserve sufficient unity and determination to maintain these barriers indefinitely. Many Germans, indeed, relished the fact that so many people in the victor nations, particularly in Britain, shared their own conviction that the "Carthaginian" settlement had been unjust. The lack of self-confidence of the defenders of the peace settlement, particularly France, is well reflected in their famous "pactomania"—the forlorn effort to conceal unfavorable power relationships behind a thick foliage of paper guarantees.

An Impermanent 'Normalcy'

Since this Indian summer of the old system was the "normalcy" to which those who fought World War II referred in thinking about the postwar world, it is essential to understand the impermanence which marked it from the start.

1. Britain and France were left as the only great powers in Europe. But France had lost nearly 1.4 million dead in the war, Britain about 750,000. Both had divested themselves of a good deal of their overseas investment to pay for the war. Both were even more wounded psychologically, and increasingly reluctant to contemplate renewed hostilities. Finally, their policies in the 1920s and 1930s were usually at cross purposes. At first France

tried to enforce the peace treaty to the letter. The collapse of that effort in the face of German passive resistance and inflation led France, step by step, into dependence on Britain. With the Locarno pact of 1925 the French followed the British in an effort to conciliate Germany, albeit within the postwar status quo.

2. Germany remained aware of its strength. The German population had grown to over 68 million by 1938 (not including Austria), while Britain had 48 million and France, less than 42 million. Germany's preponderance, as before 1914, was equally marked in general industrial strength and steel production. Although the Versailles Treaty's main limits remained intact through the 1920s, a number of improvements the Weimar Republic obtained in those years gave it reason to hope that the remaining limits might be modified or abolished in time. The Locarno arrangement in particular was something of a triumph for German diplomacy in that it advertised the British refusal to make a guarantee to France's allies on Germany's eastern border.

3. Between Germany and Soviet Russia lay a bank of new or revived countries whose lands had for centuries belonged either to these two states or to Austria or Turkey. The independence of these states derived from the disappearance of Austria-Hungary and the enfeeblement of both Germany and Russia. Poland was considered almost a great power, and the Little Entente of Czechoslovakia, Yugoslavia and Rumania had a similar status. All were allied to France in defense of the postwar settlement.

4. The Soviet Union emerged from its isolation in 1922 at Rapallo to establish a kind of *entente* with Germany, and thus facilitated reconciliation between Germany and the victorious allies, who feared that the two great "outcasts" might unite to upset the peace.

What were the chances for survival of this system? It is overly deterministic to be certain that World War II and its sequels were all quite inevitable. Nevertheless, two things are sure: first, that both Germany and Russia were profoundly anti-status quo, and second, that the sum of their potential power was much greater than the sum of the power of those European countries that were pro-status quo.

Although this was not so clear to contemporaries, in the long run the status quo was bound to be changed. A review of the history of the Weimar Republic suggests that even a prosperous Germany would have been unlikely to be content with equality within the Versailles system and frontiers. This is borne out by the career of Gustav Stresemann, German foreign minister from 1923 until his death in 1929 and principal architect of the policy of "fulfillment" of the Versailles terms: his uphill struggle to carry his own conservative party along with his policy; his connivance at clandestine German rearmament; above all his care

The Bettmann Archive, Inc.

In 1918 Poland reappeared on the European map for the first time since 1795. Józef Pilsudski, a national hero, was the first head of state and commander-in-chief of the Polish army.

to keep Germany's claims and options open in the East.

For it was above all the Polish frontier which was the fixed target of German revisionists. No German government was likely to overlook the obvious facts that Poland and the other Eastern states were weak and that Germany was in a position to pursue revisionism in the East either in partnership with the Soviet Union (the Rapallo option) or with the acquiescence if not the support of the Western powers (and particularly of Britain), perhaps in the name of defense against Bolshevism.

In any event, if anything was inevitable it was the impact of the great depression on Germany. U.S. policy—actions and nonactions—contributed mightily to its length and severity, without which Hitler almost certainly would not have come to power. The economic interdependence of the 1920s led on, step by step, to crisis, war and postwar interdependence. Nothing is recent, fortuitous, or transitory about this. The United States has been involved in Europe's fate every step of the way.

The Western allies had opportunities in the late 1930s which they could have used better. But the countries that had failed to partition Germany in 1919 could hardly have avoided the eventual consequences of German power even if Hitler had never come to power or had been deposed before the war began. The outcome might have been a very different kind of German hegemony than Hitler's, but there is no sign of the economic, demographic or diplomatic revolution in Europe that would have been necessary to modify the fact of German supremacy. Germany, having lost the war, was ready and able to challenge the outcome; Britain and France, having won, were not ready to defend it.

The Road to War

The actual course of events after 1933 was straightforward—to war. As long as the German army was small, French military predominance gave Poland and the other Eastern states their chance to live. But in March 1935 Hitler renounced the Versailles limitations and began to rearm on a large scale. As long as the Rhineland remained demilitarized, the French were able, in theory at least, to sweep into the heart of Germany if

Germany moved against the East. But in March 1936 Hitler remilitarized the Rhineland, without response from the Western powers. This—and not Munich—was the crisis of the decade. From that moment the Eastern states could not be saved from German attack without a major war.

The British government continued to hope, into 1939, that an overall agreement might satisfy Germany's "legitimate" grievances in Europe—including, in particular, the implementation of the Wilsonian principle of nationality in favor of Germans residing in Austria, Czechoslovakia and Poland. The French did not share these hopes but after 1936 were incapable of an independent policy line. These circumstances led in September 1938 to the Munich Agreement partitioning Czechoslovakia and, with Hitler's success, to the aborting of the most serious prewar plan made in Germany to depose him.

In March 1939, Germany seized what remained of Czechoslovakia after Munich. This act galvanized the British into issuing a unilateral guarantee of Poland, obviously the next object of German policy. Britain and France also pursued desultory negotiations with the Soviet Union, whose offers of an alliance they had done little to test.

Talks also began in the late spring between the Soviet Union and Germany. On August 23 the two signed a nonaggression pact including a secret protocol providing for the partition of Poland and all Eastern Europe between them. Britain's sudden guarantee of Poland did nothing for Poland, which was overrun by Germany and the U.S.S.R. within a month, but it sufficed to bring Britain and France into war when Hitler moved east on September 1. In the spring of 1940 Germany overran Norway, Denmark, Holland and Belgium, and, to the surprise even of some Germans, defeated France in a few weeks. Britain remained fighting, not for its postwar cohegemony of Europe, but for its existence as an independent state.

What almost happened in 1918, but for American intervention, happened in 1940. This time the United States had either to live with these results or make a far greater effort than before, with far greater consequences for itself and Europe, to reverse them.

3

World War II: From One System to Another

World War II completed the transformation of the European power scale that had been under way since 1870. As a result of decisions made by Britain, the Soviet Union and the United States during the war, the Germany created in 1871 was not merely weakened as a factor in European affairs, as in 1919, but was destroyed as a state. Its disappearance left all of Europe subject to the three countries which controlled decisive power when the war ended. Their relations, in turn, were conditioned by military and diplomatic events of World War II which were the determinants of postwar Europe.

After defeating France in June 1940, the Germans extended their rule over the Balkans as a prelude to their attack on the Soviet Union in June 1941. Despite very heavy Allied setbacks in the Pacific and in Russia during 1942, American entry into the war in December 1941 meant that neither Britain nor the U.S.S.R. would be defeated as France had been. But the enormity of the military problems was such that it took the allies two and one-half years after the United States entered the war to land in France. The delay was to become a serious source of wartime friction—the Russians fearing that the United States

Wide World Photos

Adolf Hitler performed this joyous little dance at Compiegne in 1940 after dictating armistice terms to conquered France.

and Britain might wish to see Germany and the U.S.S.R. fight on indefinitely, and the West concerned that the Russians, believing this, might contemplate a separate peace.

In November 1942 the Western allies took the offensive in French North Africa, defeating German and Italian forces in May 1943. While this fighting was still going on, Franklin D. Roosevelt and Winston Churchill met at Casablanca in January 1943. There they decided to ask unconditional surrender of the Axis powers. This was seen as a self-denying ordinance against the possibility of a separate peace, as well as a public pledge that a second front in Europe would be launched. Most important, it was intended to make clear to the Germans that the allies intended to deal with Germany after the war with a free hand.

Unconditional surrender has been criticized on the grounds that it strengthened German resolve to fight and discouraged dissident groups that might have overthrown Hitler and made peace. This is an unrealistic kind of *realpolitik*. If the war had ended with a still-united, assertive, powerful, by no means acquiescent Germany led by the anti-Hitler plotters of July 1944, would that necessarily have been better for Europe than the West Germany that emerged after 1949, purged by total defeat of its internal demons and no longer able, even if it wished, to pursue disruptive goals? The Casablanca formula opened the door to the possibility of settling the German problem once and for all—and that, after all, was what the war in Europe was all about.

The unconditional surrender formula, designed to fit the German case, was applied less than literally against Italy and Japan, the other two major Axis powers. When the British and Americans invaded Sicily in July 1943, King Victor Emmanuel III of Italy dismissed Mussolini and formed a new government under Marshal Pietro Badoglio. The allies then accepted the surrender of this regime. Thereupon the Soviet Union asked for a three-power Allied commission, including itself, to supervise the occupation of Italy. The Western allies successfully resisted this proposal on the ground that, as Churchill put it, they were "doing all the fighting."

The Russians Enter Eastern Europe

The principle thus established in Italy was next applied by the Russians themselves in Eastern Europe. In the summer of 1944 the Red Army began to move across the 1939 frontiers of the Soviet Union. When the Red Army entered Rumania and Bulgaria and dictated armistices to both, all effective power was vested in the Soviet military commander. Later the Russians, whose troops were "doing all the fighting" in these countries, cited the Italian armistice regime as the precedent.

Watching this Russian advance into the Balkans, Churchill decided to try for a frank spheres-of-influence deal with Stalin. Since he knew the strong American objection to the concept,

Churchill claimed to be concerned only about short-term military arrangements, and on this basis Roosevelt sanctioned a three-month trial. Churchill went to Moscow in October 1944 and made his proposal to Stalin on a slip of paper. Stalin at once accepted it. In Rumania and Bulgaria, the U.S.S.R. was to have predominant influence, the West a minor share; in Greece the situation was to be the reverse. In Yugoslavia and Hungary it was to be 50-50. Poland, the most difficult case, was not included.

During the 1950s Churchill was widely credited—by Roosevelt's detractors—with having tried to get the Western allies to move militarily into the Balkans and Central Europe to prevent the Soviet Union from establishing control. It is true that for a few weeks in the summer of 1944 Churchill wanted the British-led army of Italy to march from Rome through Yugoslavia to Vienna—an idea whose practicality was more than questionable. At other times he had quite different reasons for promoting military activity in the Mediterranean area and doing what he could to put off an Allied landing in France which was expected to exact a fearful toll of Allied casualties. When the American military leaders insisted that the main business was landing in France and marching to the heartland of German power, Churchill never pressed the issue to a decisive showdown on the grounds of heading off the Soviet conquest of Eastern Europe, or any other.

Much of the discussion of this issue seems to take for granted that the United States could have done anything it wished whereas the Russians were weak. Such assumptions are absurd. The United States was very strong at war's end but not omnipotent. The victorious Red Army was a formidable instrument. It must be said here, because it underlies so much of what follows, that the Soviet Union won the war too.

What can be validly criticized is the American government's failure to follow Churchill's example to try to work out what terms it could get for the area from the Russians. But Roosevelt purposely tried to keep American hands free of specific postwar territorial agreements, and as far as possible to keep Britain free also.

Occupation of Defeated Germany

When the British and Americans finally landed on the coast of France on June 6, 1944, they did so in such power that their initial advance was very much quicker and less bloody than had been expected. France was practically cleared of the Germans by year's end. Germany was gradually occupied by the armies advancing from east and west, and it surrendered unconditionally on May 7, 1945.

The allies had long taken for granted that, consistent with unconditional surrender, they would occupy Germany, and they began to negotiate about the relevant problems soon after the Casablanca conference. The zonal agreement and occupation plans were finally approved at Yalta, in February 1945. They provided for military occupation in prescribed zones, joint occupation of Berlin in three sectors, and an Allied Control Council to make policy for all of Germany, composed of the commanders-in-chief and operating by unanimous agreement.

One other important decision was made at Yalta: the inclusion of France in the plans for the occupation of Germany. By then the British, thinking that the Americans would not stay on in Germany for very long, had become convinced that France should take part in the occupation. It was agreed that the French zone would be carved entirely from territory assigned to the other two Western powers, and that France would join the Allied Control Council as an equal member.

As it turned out, the Western armies moved east into Germany beyond their zonal boundaries before the war ended. Churchill urged the American government to let the Western allies hold their ground and not implement the occupation agreements until the Russians made concessions on disputed matters in Eastern Europe. But the United States was eager to implement the control machinery in Germany and concluded that it was necessary to abide by the agreed zonal lines. By July the occupation of Germany and of Berlin by the four powers had been put into place. Only then, at Potsdam, did the Big Three make their first systematic attempt to decide what to do with the country—no longer a state—whose sovereignty they had jointly assumed.

4

Entrance of the Superpowers

The power of the two great peripheral states that had taken a less than central part in European affairs before 1939 was revealed, if not in a sense created, by the war. By mid-1945 they (along with Britain) were in control of all Europe. The revived European states at once found themselves involved in a new power system that had its roots in events of the preceding 60 or 70 years, but had no resemblance to the old multipolar, European-centered system.

The most important and persistent theme in European affairs from then to now has been the continuous interplay between the United States and the Soviet Union. These two great states, alone of their kind in the world, were left face to face in Central Europe with a starkness, from the point of view of *power,* that is still not fully grasped. The problem is not to explain why there was friction between them, which should have been expected in the circumstances, but to understand why their relations took the particular contentious direction they did.

The Soviet Union

Understanding of Soviet foreign policy is severely hobbled by the scarcity of relevant documents. This situation requires, but has not produced, the utmost prudence in drawing conclusions. The mainstream of Western analysis during the cold war period saw Soviet policy as deeply purposeful, devious and expansionist—in the typology of William Welch's *American Images of Soviet Foreign Policy,* as the Great Beast of Revelation. More recently, the Soviet Union has sometimes emerged from between the lines of American revisionism as an Injured Lamb.

The model I suggest here might be called simply the Other Superpower. It assumes that Soviet policy has been the work of politicians and diplomats as well as ideologues, pursuing discrete and finite goals as well as others that were less so. But on some important points the only sound conclusion in the light of grossly deficient data must be the Scottish verdict of "not proven."

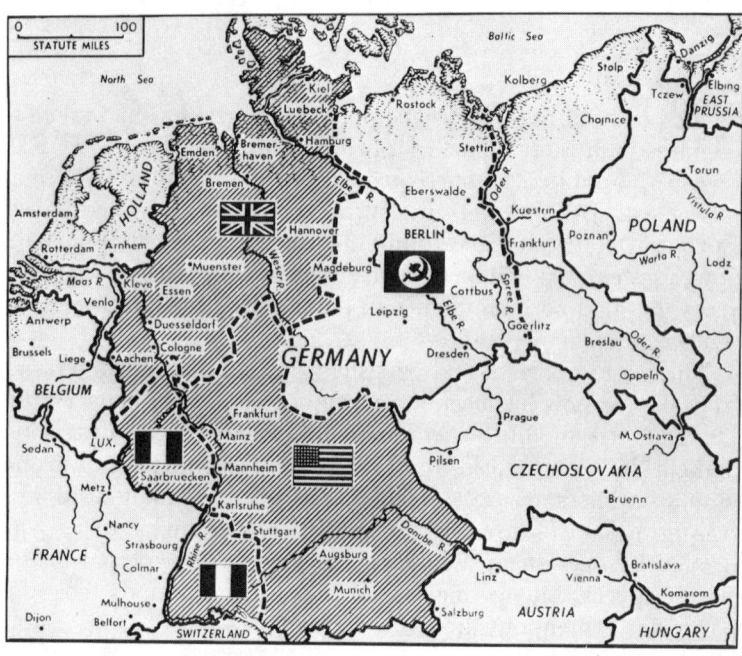

Wide World Photos

The postwar division of Germany, on which the East-West balance in Europe rests, had its origin in the military occupation zones established as World War II ended.

In the Soviet Union, as in every country, foreign policy is colored by geography and history. No Russian government in 1945 would be oblivious to where its frontier was fixed. Nor would any Russian government overlook Russia's historic frontiers, brutally changed between 1918 and 1920 in one of the country's darkest hours. In this sense, any Russian government would see 1945 as belated justice for 1918.

At the same time, the ideological background of the Russian rulers is an important input into their foreign policy, coloring their thinking about and interpretation of events and the policies of others. The Bolshevik leaders of 1917-18 believed that their success was only the first phase of a general revolution. By 1920 or 1921, however, finding themselves in control of the one and only "socialist" country in the world, they had to accept the fact that they were going to live for a while in a world of capitalist states. That did not mean that they gave up their Marxist-Leninist view of the world or, above all, their clear-cut notion that the U.S.S.R. lived in a world of states which were profoundly hostile.

The Soviet leaders thus proceeded with both confidence and caution in the face of the obvious power of the United States. But the tone and turn Stalin gave to Soviet society had an important impact on other countries. His repressive measures at home were similar enough to those of the well-remembered Nazi system to lead many to think that his foreign policy was also Hitlerian. It is easy to see how Western contemporaries of Stalin overlooked the practical prudence behind the harsh rhetoric which filled the air in those years, and drew the worst conclusions from the forced communization of the states of Eastern Europe and the activities of the Western Communist parties from 1945 on. However, it was probably mistaken to conclude that Stalin's regime was as disposed as Hitler's to risk war in pursuit of its goals. Hitler thought that he was working with destiny because of the might of the *present* German state; the Soviet Communists believed that history was on their side whatever the immediate constellation of power in the world. Very different policies followed from these beliefs.

The main specific elements of Soviet policy in 1945 and

in the years that followed may be summed up this way:

1. The first requirement was to establish what were then thought to be secure frontiers. The new line, from Finland south to Rumania, was not in the end the 1914 Russian frontier because Finland and Poland survived as independent states. But it was close, and represented to the Soviet leaders their coming back into possession of those Russian lands of which they had been despoiled in 1918 and, after a brief reoccupation, in 1941.

2. Any victorious Russian government would have wanted "friendly" states across the border. Did Stalin see any alternative to an anti-Soviet *cordon sanitaire* other than satellization? The answer appears to have been affirmative in the case of Finland, negative in the cases of Poland and Rumania. These two countries were strongly anti-Russian between the wars and both had just lost much territory to it. It is therefore plausible to think that Stalin had decided early to impose regimes in Poland, and probably also in Rumania, which would be friendly to the U.S.S.R. not only because of ideological ties but also because of their weak domestic support.

Bulgaria's satellization must have seemed less necessary but nevertheless a natural and easy revival of a Russian policy dating from the 1870s and a means of bringing added influence to bear on Turkey and perhaps also on Yugoslavia. As for Hungary and Czechoslovakia, it is unclear whether the Russians proceeded according to an advance plan there, but only as fast as they judged internal and Western resistance would permit, or whether the communization of these countries came about as part of a process of interacting events between the U.S.S.R. and the Western powers in the 1945-48 period.

3. The Soviet leaders wanted to make sure that Germany did not renew its aggression, either alone or as part of an anti-Soviet bloc. Their obsession with Germany long remained out of proportion to the threat posed to the U.S.S.R., now a global superpower.

Germany's most important industrial resources were in the zones occupied by the Western powers. That implied that the U.S.S.R. had to cooperate with them if it was to gain substantial industrial reparations in the short term and have a voice in the disposition of Germany in the long. But the Russians also became increasingly committed to keeping control of the resources—and the future development—of their own zone of occupation. We do not know just when they decided to sacrifice the former priority to the latter.

4. There is reason to think that the Soviet leaders did not exclude cooperation with the other major allies in Germany *a priori* and in fact saw certain benefits in it but also that there were policy goals that took priority if they had to make such a choice. Their *sine qua non* for this cooperation was Western acceptance of the priority goals of Soviet policy I have discussed. When that was denied, the possibility of maintaining even a facade of cooperation disappeared.

5. Beyond its territorial, hegemonic, and security policies, the Soviet Union had a wider goal: to have its frontiers and sphere of influence recognized by the other great powers. An even broader goal was to be treated by the Western allies as a great power. In this, as in other things, Russian nationalism was at work. It led the Russians, for example, to claim trusteeship over a former Italian colony in Africa.

This Soviet demand struck the Western leaders as sinister. The episode highlights the deeper problem of Soviet claims to, and Western reluctance to accept, the full implications in status terms of the U.S.S.R.'s position as a *world* power. What did the victory won at such enormous cost amount to, the Russians might have asked, if not recognition of Soviet claims and interests by those powers which had sacrificed less? If the United States could establish outposts in Central Europe and Japan, why could not the Russians express their interest in areas beyond their traditional sphere? The West continues to find it not only disquieting, which is natural, but odd, which is less understandable, that the co-victor of World War II asserts global interests and has gradually developed a global reach.

6. One means by which the Russians hoped to exert influence in areas outside their military control was the Communist parties of the West, which in 1945 shared power in many European countries. As long as Communists remained in Western govern-

ments, such countries could not take part in a bloc hostile to the U.S.S.R. Even out of office the Communist parties might hope to prevent these countries from becoming actively anti-Soviet. Whether the Russians saw them as having serious prospects of taking over control of these Western countries is less certain.

The United States

For all its continuous involvement with European civilization, there has been a kind of national impatience in America with the tiresome and dangerous complexities of European history and politics, an impatience reinforced by the happy fact that the United States had been able to develop at a long distance from powerful neighbors and had a history of only sporadic conflict with other countries. This had the important consequence of inculcating the idea that military and political rivalry among nations need not be the law of life and that order and security are the normal course of things. All this, of course, is the reverse of the European experience—not least the Russian.

A further implication has been the long-held notion that the United States was not a *regular* participant in world affairs but intervenes only in great emergencies and, in those cases, sets its foreign policy goals in high and abstract terms.

Roosevelt, along with Secretary of State Cordell Hull and many others, shared Wilson's antipathy to traditional European politics, to alliances and balance of power, to militarism and colonialism—all the things which they thought, not without reason, had led to war. They believed that America's good was good for all men and that America's interests were naturally the same as those of all nations. The Roosevelt Administration moved along a slow path from the isolationism of the mid-30s, but once Roosevelt decided that the United States must prevent a German victory, he understood that a U.S.-British victory would have to bring more than a return to the status quo ante.

Serious attention was given first to economic problems. It was widely accepted in the United States and elsewhere that an important underlying cause of German and Japanese aggression was the economic depression and the policies that had contributed to it and stemmed from it, including high tariffs, competitive devaluations and cartel agreements. Freer trade meant greater prosperity for all, prosperity meant—eventually at least—democracy, democracy meant peace. These beliefs underlay repeated pledges of nondiscriminatory trade policy exacted from Britain, and to the agreement in 1944 to found the International Bank for Reconstruction and Development and the International Monetary Fund (IMF).

The political side of the American design for the postwar world came to be centered officially on the United Nations. The world security system was to be built on the continued harmony of the principal wartime allies, those that Roosevelt called the Four Policemen: the United States, the Soviet Union, Britain and China. Peace in the future would depend on the prompt use of force against peacebreakers, and only the great powers possessed such force. The permanent members of the Security Council, therefore, were armed with a veto.

The organization had the symbolic purpose of committing the United States to continuous participation in world affairs in a form that was alleged to be very different from the old balance-of-power system. Behind it, nevertheless, was a realistic attempt to achieve some degree of world order by concertation among the major powers, at least to the extent of preventing major war. That attempt may have been bound to fail initially because each superpower saw an ideological threat in the other rather than, as after 1815, in a defeated but still powerful enemy. Curiously, the military uses of atomic energy emerged just then to provide the common threat that, after a long detour of hostile confrontation, prompted the beginning of *détente*.

Even during the war there were many Americans, not excluding many in the government, who remained fundamentally anti-Communist and anti-Soviet, and were skeptical or worse about the chances for U.S.-Soviet cooperation when peace came. But Roosevelt's view of the world did not include anti-Bolshevism. To Roosevelt the ideological division of World War II was militarist Germany and its allies on one side, all its enemies on the other. Business could be done with the latter but not the former.

Once the tide of war had turned, Roosevelt held to this basic line of dealing with the Russians. In his view the Soviet Union was needed for the peace just as it had been for the war. One important tactic, his policy of putting off decisions on territorial questions until the end of the war, was challenged by the Russians, who wanted acceptance of the frontiers they sought in Eastern Europe, and also by the British, who understood that their own relative power would wane rapidly after the war ended.

No American at the decision-making level saw the merit, as Churchill did, of striking the best deal possible with the Russians as the preface to establishing the postwar order. Certainly no one thought of an understanding on spheres of influence as a prerequisite to doing so. Just before he died, Roosevelt began to express concern about Soviet policies, particularly in Poland. Whatever he might have done, had he lived, about the situation the United States confronted at the end of the war in Europe, we know that his successor, Harry Truman, and the Soviet government together participated in a series of events which led to the cold war.

Certainly an elaborate international structure where some deference was paid to the interests of lesser states was not the Soviet vision of the future. The Russians could not have been expected to take the formal framework of the UN very seriously, nor to have been unwary of a body which, at its inception, was bound to be under the control of capitalist states. To them both the organization and the great power directorate which lay behind it had to reflect, not supersede, the respective spheres and interests of the main powers.

But the United States did not accept that its conception of the postwar world would have to be adjusted to the interests of a powerful co-victor. It did not accept the manner or the outcome of Soviet policy in Poland and Rumania. It did not accept the creation of a closed economic bloc in Eastern Europe. Above all, the Americans refused to accept that the UN and its great-power directorate might be built on a system of spheres of influence.

Accordingly, the United States made an effort to change Soviet policy. The Polish problem was the occasion for this effort. Its failure launched the cold war.

5
The Cold War Begins

Louis J. Halle, in his book *The Cold War as History,* correctly observed that "there is a sense in which the cold war, like World War II, began with a Western attempt to rescue a Poland that was beyond its reach." If the Big Three had not fallen out in early 1945 over the Polish question, they might well have done so on some other issue. But their first great quarrel was about the frontiers and the government of Poland, and the circumstances of that quarrel colored their relations thereafter in a particular way.

The Clash Over Poland

It is not surprising that the Polish question became for the United States a touchstone of Soviet cooperativeness. By 1945 the United States had been through more than three years of war fought in the name of principles it took seriously; had designed plans for a postwar world on a scale proportional to the effort made in winning the war; and had become a global power unwilling to be excluded from presence and influence in any part of the world.

It is even less surprising that the Russian leaders saw this matter as a touchstone of Western attitudes toward *them*. Poland had been partitioned between Germany and Russia in 1939, but when war broke out between them in June 1941 the Germans quickly overran the rest of the country. Russian leaders emphasized to their allies that they expected to regain that part of Poland which they had seized in 1939. They made much of the fact that most of the area they claimed had been assigned to them by an Allied commission in 1919 but then was forcibly seized by the new Polish state. At Teheran in December 1943, Churchill agreed to accept this so-called Curzon line. Roosevelt did not agree. Nothing was put in writing, but from Stalin's point of view the matter must have seemed settled.

By then the question of frontiers had given way to the more important issue of who was to rule Poland. The Soviet government had established diplomatic relations with the Polish government-in-exile in London. But in 1943, when the Germans accused the Soviets of murdering the 10,000 Polish officers whose bodies they found in the Katyn Forest in Russia, the London Poles asked the Red Cross to investigate. The Russians, claiming that this meant that the government-in-exile gave credence to the charge, broke diplomatic relations with it. They were never reestablished.

Even before this break the Russians had set up a Moscow group called the Union of Polish Patriots, mostly but not all Communists. In July 1944 it was established in Lublin as the Polish Committee of National Liberation. On the last day of 1944 the committee retitled itself the provisional government of Poland, and on January 5, 1945, the Soviet Union recognized it.

It should have been obvious from the start that, unless the Western allies wanted to fight the Soviet Union, power in Poland would go to the protégés of the Red Army. The only options open to the allies were to swallow the *fait accompli* or to challenge what the Russians were doing. In neither case could they expect to have any appreciable impact on events in Poland.

Much of the Yalta conference was taken up with haggling about how to put the London and Warsaw Polish groups together in one provisional government which all the allies could recognize. The legislative history and the actual wording of the understanding finally reached leave no doubt that the Big Three intended that the provisional government then functioning in Warsaw was to be reorganized into a new Provisional Government of National Unity by the addition of other Poles, including some from the London group. But the balance clearly lay toward Lublin.

It is hard to believe that Roosevelt and Churchill did not know how widely different were their intentions from Stalin's. But they also knew what they were doing when they settled for the enlargement of the Lublin government. Presumably they thought that the elections promised by Stalin would permit something other than a purely Communist government to emerge. This was, as Churchill said, the best they could get. The same hope-against-hope reasoning applied to the rest of Eastern Europe no doubt lay behind their support of the vague Declaration on Liberated Europe.

Truman's Early Policies

Roosevelt died in April 1945, and the new Truman Administration quickly adopted a firm attitude toward what it saw as Soviet violations of Allied agreements. Yet the American government's new firmness was erratic. The United States practically abandoned its case on Polish affairs as part of an arrangement which also included Soviet concessions on UN issues. Then in June 1945 Washington suddenly took up the cudgels against Russian policy in Rumania and Bulgaria, only to give up active interest in these countries as part of a comprehensive agreement with the Soviet Union concluded in December at a three-power meeting in Moscow.

Soviet purposes are clear with respect both to frontiers and to the overriding importance the Russians attached to the nature of the postwar Polish regime. The British position was also quite clear. It is harder to get a fully satisfying grasp on the American position. But the objective of obtaining at least a minimal role in Eastern Europe inspired much of American policy toward that area through 1945. It did not necessarily contradict Soviet predominance, but it refused to accept Soviet exclusivity.

Truman's Administration was more resentful of Soviet unilateralism in Poland than Roosevelt's, linking it with what seemed to be comparable acts elsewhere and adding them all up into a pattern of actual and potential Soviet expansionism to which American firmness was seen as the only reply.

It has been argued that the Americans carefully planned to use their possession of the atomic bomb to intimidate the Soviet Union on Balkan issues. But we can wonder whether American leaders did have such a diplomatic strategy, for if so, they played this card with a lack of skill incredibly out of proportion to the supposed subtlety of the prior preparation. The bomb had no discernible impact in 1945 on Eastern Europe unless its possession led the American government to yield to domestic pressures for demobilizing in Europe more promptly than might otherwise have been the case, thereby weakening rather than strengthening the U.S. diplomatic hand.

It has also been suggested that the new American administration took for granted that the Soviet Union desperately needed economic help for reconstruction and would pay a high price with respect to Eastern Europe and other issues to get it. The unreadiness of Congress to consider substantial postwar aid to the allies and Truman's determination to get tough with the Russians led to the decisions which the Russians had reason to see as attempts to use economic leverage.

The first decision was to cut off immediately lend-lease to the Soviet Union after V-E day. The second was the back-off of the United States from the agreement made at Yalta regarding reparations from Germany so that the compromise finally worked out at Potsdam fell far short of Soviet expectations. The third issue concerned the Soviet application in January 1945 for a $6 billion loan. The American government, after a long delay, apparently decided to try to use the loan application as explicit leverage on a wide range of Soviet foreign policies. But the Russians refused to accept much of the agenda proposed by Washington, and no negotiations took place.

The assumption that their need for help could have pried meaningful concessions from the Russians might have been correct in the early years of the war, but in 1945 it was simply

1949: Cartoonist Edwin Marcus expressed a widely held U.S. view of Soviet policy in the postwar world. As the figure of an accusing Stalin implies, the Soviet view of U.S. policy was equally hostile.

Marcus, © 1949 by the New York Times Co. Reprinted by permission.

wrong. The Russians had their own illusions on the subject, believing that the United States needed them as customers to avert a depression and would therefore provide credits on easy terms and with no strings. In any case, the assumed American leverage was wildly inadequate to the objectives set for it.

For the United States, the most important result of the wrangling with the Soviet Union about Poland and the Balkans was to sensitize American opinion to what the Soviet Union was doing in Eastern Europe. That, building on latent anti-Bolshevism, gave a powerful impetus to the oncoming cold war psychology in the United States.

The Soviet Response

It is less clear what effect these events had on Soviet policy. We can set aside the once popular notion that the Russian leaders followed some kind of blueprint or timetable for expansion beyond the gains which the war brought them. On the other hand, there is no reason to assume that the Russians were ready for an openhanded postwar partnership with Britain and the United States but were turned aside from it by Western policy.

This said, we are entitled to speculate about the way American policies may have interacted with what seem to have been the priorities of Soviet policy as the war ended. In light of the Churchill-Stalin spheres of influence deal and the handling of the Polish question at Yalta, Stalin had reason to think that his grip on Poland and much of Eastern Europe had been recognized, or at least acquiesced in, by the Western allies. Subsequent Allied efforts to influence the affairs of the area probably seemed to him to reflect a shift to a more hostile position toward the Soviet Union. The significance of the change may have seemed the greater in that it coincided with a new American administration. The atomic weapon was also a fearful if ambiguous addition to the calculus of power.

These considerations do not prove that the Soviet leaders were driven by American policy from a course of likely cooperation with the West to one of cold war. They do indicate that whatever chance there was that the Russians might have continued to find it in their interest to collaborate with the West for certain purposes was reduced by the policy interactions of 1945.

For the United States, it was but a step from treating the Soviet sphere in Eastern Europe as illegitimate to seeing all Soviet activities in world affairs as equally illegitimate and aggressive. For the Russians it was but a step from seeing the United States challenge the fruits of their hard-won victory in the area of greatest importance to their security to seeing an American effort to encircle and perhaps extirpate the homeland of socialism.

The competition between the superpowers in due course would attach itself to or even create conflicts in every corner of the world before the two powers returned, after a disrupted quarter-century, to a second effort to achieve at least some relaxation of systematic tension, if not a new form of entente. Between these two attempts to define American-Soviet relations in some way other than total hostile competition lies the cold war.

6

The Building of a New State System

The two superpowers, meeting each other seriously for the first time, and as the co-arbiters of Europe, might have worked out their mutual relations in any of several possible ways. For reasons stemming from history, ideological preconceptions, and the actual circumstances they faced in Europe, the meeting was hostile rather than collaborative. But in the end they *did* establish the bases of a relationship in Europe within which they could live together without war, but almost without realizing that they were doing so.

The meaning of the cold war has thus turned out to be a search by the two superpowers for a means to define their relations to each other in such a way as to assure the survival of both themselves and the countries grouped around them. The system of states which finally came into being represents the first stable set of relationships Europe has known since the rise of German power.

This stability, of course, is a relative thing, and much has happened in Europe within the bipolar structure. It is also true that for the European states the new system is basically worldwide and therefore no longer theirs. For the superpowers themselves, the creative stabilization of their competition in Europe is still imperfect in the absence of a yet to be achieved worldwide stabilization—and in the world, other forces at play may be too powerful to be stabilized by anything the United States and the Soviet Union can do.

The new European system has preserved the national independence of the member states, though severely circumscribed in the case of the Soviet Union's dependents. It has kept the peace, too. Since it has reflected the distribution of power in Europe, it has already maintained its distinctive form over a considerable period. It is clearly not a way station back to the earlier system. But neither is it necessarily a way station forward to some other system.

From Poland to Containment

The process of working out the relationship of the superpowers in Europe began with the imposition of Soviet control in Poland and other Eastern European countries. This took considerable time, constantly providing Americans and other Westerners new evidence of Soviet expansionism. The game in Poland itself was not played out in 1945. Stanislaw Mikolajczyk and a few of his associates entered the Communist-dominated Polish government in the summer and lingered on in Poland until as late as October 1947, but his eventual departure made no difference to the fait accompli of Communist control. The establishment of a full-fledged people's democracy in Rumania in the following April only advertised another fait accompli. In Bulgaria the Communists and their associates took full power even more readily.

Reasonably free elections took place in Hungary and Czechoslovakia in 1945 and 1946, respectively, and governments were established which were not dominated by the Communist participants. But in the August 1947 election in Hungary the Communists won control of parliament and the government which they then transformed into total control. In Czechoslovakia a cabinet dispute led the non-Communist ministers in the coalition government to resign in February 1948. President Eduard Beneš accepted a new cabinet dominated by Communists. These events, climaxed by Foreign Minister Jan Masaryk's death, marked the end of democracy in the first and last country of Eastern Europe to have enjoyed it.

Sensitized to what the Soviet Union was doing in Eastern Europe, American public and official thinking moved steadily but not unswervingly toward hostile confrontation with the Soviet Union. The drawn-out debate in 1946-47 over the atomic problem, culminating in the Soviet rejection of the American plan for international control of atomic weapons, further envenomed emerging cold war tension.

But when Truman went before Congress in March 1947 to urge that the United States pick up the burden that the British were dropping of sustaining Greece against internal subversion and assume its own burden of helping Turkey resist possible external aggression, he found it useful to present the issues with utmost sharpness. Without naming Russia or Communism as the villain, Truman described a worldwide struggle between two ways of life, one based on the will of the majority and free institutions, the other forcibly imposed by a minority and based on oppression and terror.

Truman tried to make the issue posed by the immediate crisis so clear to his fellow countrymen that they could constantly and readily reapply it to many other situations. This distinction between those whom the United States chose to support and those whom it found to be threatening them and itself provided an easy, almost mechanical definition of national interest. American foreign policy thinking, official and public, became and long remained dichotomous.

The policy line expressed by Truman—which came to be known as the Truman Doctrine—was expounded in a more sophisticated manner by George Kennan, in his renowned *Foreign Affairs* article, signed X, of July 1947. According to Kennan, the Western response to Soviet "pressure" should be "firm and vigilant containment." Containment, the historian Bruce Kuklick has written, was the American grand design for the postwar world scaled down to reality. If the Soviet Union would not cooperate willingly and if it could not be coerced into cooperation, then there was nothing to do but go ahead without it and organize as much of the world as was available.

The Marshall Plan: Europe Divides

On the political side, both the means and the ends of policy had to be found, and they were. On the economic side, the former global goals were retained but new policies had to be developed to promote them in the unforeseen conditions of the late 1940s. The United States had tried since before the end of the war to implement its economic design with the countries outside the emerging Soviet bloc. But it had met one disappointment after another. A firm economic base was not established capable of either maintaining stability or making possible the open door economic system the United States wanted. It was believed on both sides of the Atlantic that economic distress would lead to social and political breakdown and that, in turn, to a situation which the Soviet Union would not fail to take advantage of.

Beginning in March 1947, therefore, the Truman Administration began to plan a response addressed not only to the immediate situation but also to the economic roots of the problem. Secretary

Wide World Photos

The Age of Bipartisanship: Senate leaders Arthur H. Vandenberg (R.-Mich.) (l.) and Tom Connally (D-Tex.) (r.) conferred in February 1947 with Secretary of State George C. Marshall.

of State George C. Marshall, in his speech at Harvard on June 5, proposed long-term American grant aid to a cooperative European regional economic effort. The Marshall initiative and the policies that developed from it—for there was no plan at first—were at the same time continuous from the earlier American economic goals and a departure from them. The United States now accepted a long delay in currency convertibility. It was now ready to tolerate special trading and payments arrangements in Europe which it had been trying to dismantle. Indeed, it undertook to foster European economic cooperation or integration as necessary both politically and economically for a comprehensive European recovery program.

It was clear that the regional cooperation promoted by Washington concerned Western Europe, not Europe as a whole. Though the American offer was nominally open to the Soviet Union as well as to other European countries, the Russians naturally refused to join in the required cooperative response and forced their satellites to do the same, so that the onus for the division of Europe fell on them. The ensuing association in the Committee (later the Organization) for European Economic Cooperation and in the European Payments Union of the 16 European participants—plus the Anglo-American and French occupation zones in West Germany—marked the first *positive* structural delineation of the postwar division of Europe along the military line drawn in 1945.

It was not coincidental that the positive delineation of a two-bloc Europe coincided with the first attempt to define a Western European entity within the emerging American-led "Euratlantic" bloc. The new American goal of a united Western Europe had, of course, several roots. Besides economic efficiency, another was the idea that such a Europe might help attenuate old European quarrels and, above all, provide an acceptable framework for the emerging West German state.

But for the United States, Western European unity was also a most convenient component of a policy which was contributing to, or at least advertising, the division of Europe as a whole. If the traditional unity of Europe could not be restored, and if the United States itself—not to say the West Europeans—was not ready to conceive of a structured and enduring Euratlantic relationship, then the ultimate unification of Western Europe provided a rational and even emotional cause to work for beyond the exigencies of the moment. This was seen as being true for the West Germans, who had to accept the division of their country, and for the French and other neighbors of Germany, who had to accept its economic, political and, very soon, military resurrection. The eventual result was the development from 1947 on of not one but two lasting sets of institutions that defined West as against East in Europe—the Atlantic-global, first in time and rank, and, within them, the European-regional.

The structural response of the other half of Europe to the Marshall Plan and its offshoots was the formation of the Cominform in September 1947. The line of division expressed in Europe between those countries which took part in the Marshall Plan and those which joined the Cominform struck contemporaries as signifying a basic division and alignment going far beyond the actual programs of either.

But the division of Europe was not positively consummated in mid-1947, nor was the Western grouping which has emerged from that division. Both became fixed by a series of political decisions concerning the mutual security ties between the United States and the West European countries and, connected with those, the establishment and the arming of the West German state. The Anglo-French Treaty of Dunkirk (March 1947) is often seen as the first step in this process. In theory, it established the explicit mutual defense arrangement which Britain and France lacked between 1919 and 1939. In practice, it reflected the growing French conviction that France had to cover itself as best it could against a new German state whose emergence it could not prevent and whose partnership, in some form, it would have to seek.

In March 1948 the Benelux countries joined the Anglo-French alliance through the Treaty of Brussels. In July 1948 the Brussels partners entered negotiations to establish a formal alliance with the United States. Canada, Norway, Denmark, Iceland, Italy and Portugal were eventually included, and the North Atlantic Treaty was signed by the 12 founding partners on

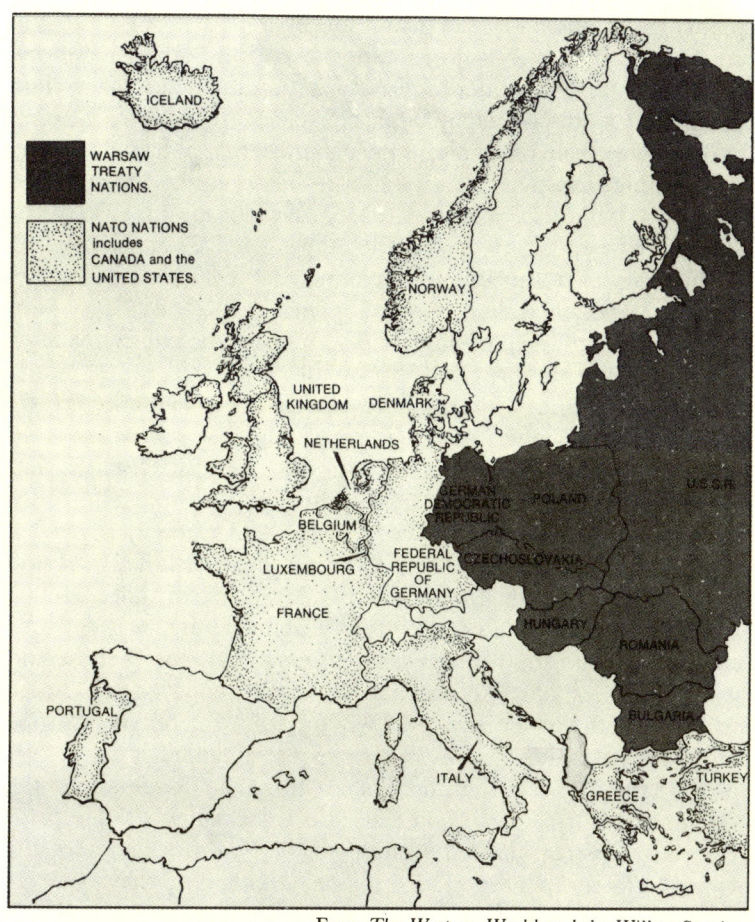

From *The Western World and the Will to Survive*,
courtesy of The Johnson Foundation

April 4, 1949. The principal objective of the arrangement was to equilibrate Soviet power in Eastern Europe by formally linking American nuclear power to the protection of Western Europe. This was the first effort to use American nuclear power in a politically explicit way.

A peacetime alliance of this kind was, of course, a striking departure from American tradition. It reflected how far the intensity of cold war feelings had carried U.S. opinion even as compared to 1947. The American commitment has over time turned out to be a fundamental choice, less in danger of being backed away from as circumstances change than of being taken as an example for other areas whose problems called for different solutions. It is also notable that few Europeans of 1949 were distressed by the fact that beneath the formal egalitarianism of the alliance lay a fundamental asymmetry: the United States gave protection and the other allies accepted it.

One of the most important implications of the choice made in 1949 was that it provided a tangible expression of a much broader community of interests which the members already shared and which was to grow increasingly comprehensive in the years to come. The North Atlantic Treaty Organization (NATO) came to be seen as a state system in itself. More accurately, the community for which NATO stood has been a component or subsystem of a system which included also the Soviet Union and its allies—that is, a state system that included almost every European state but also included and was dependent on two states that were vastly stronger than any of these and were wholly or partially extra-European.

Though the emergence of two organized blocs in Europe provided the structure of a new state system, the blocs did not yet provide stability. For that there had to be a tenable solution of the German problem which had caused the breakdown of the prior European system and led straight to the dual hegemony of the United States and the Soviet Union. Neither of these powers intended at first to bring about the German solution which emerged. Yet almost everything they did with respect to each other led to it with as great a precision as if they had planned it.

later, than the decision by the allies to arm the Federal Republic within the Western alliance. Rearmament assured, if it was not already sure, the impossibility of disentangling the now sovereign West German state from the bloc within which it was born and to which it belonged by its own choice. And once the FRG was armed, neither its allies nor its neighbors in Western and Eastern Europe nor the superpowers themselves were likely to chance setting up a power in Central Europe with both the strength to play off the two blocs against each other to its own advantage and a motive for doing so. What was true of the FRG was no less true, if not by choice, of the GDR.

German rearmament would certainly not have come about when it did, and possibly not at all, if there had been no Korean

"Der Alte" (the Old Man) was the nickname of Konrad Adenauer, first chancellor (1949–63) of the Federal Republic of Germany.

Wide World Photos

war. The aggression in Korea in June 1950 was seen as a harbinger of the same along the Elbe; or an attempt to divert American attention from Europe; or at least a testing of the viability and determination of the new Atlantic alliance, and of American commitment to it. The American policy response included an integrated alliance force in Europe, an American supreme commander, financial aid for an Allied military buildup, and sending more U.S. troops to Europe. But the American government judged that this was not enough. In September it raised with Britain and France the question of German participation in the defense of Western Europe.

Not surprisingly, the idea ran into sharp French resistance. The French government therefore proposed instead, and the Americans eventually accepted, a European Defense Community (EDC) that would include German forces but exclude national command of them or German admission directly to the alliance. But the EDC failed to win approval in the French Assembly when it finally came to a vote in August 1954.

The EDC project was a four-year education for the French to accept without subterfuge the unpalatable reality, pressed on them by the United States, of an armed and sovereign West Germany. It was also an education for the West Germans, many of whom had rejected rearmament for fear of what it might do to their infant democracy or to whatever chances there were for reunification. But Chancellor Konrad Adenauer's government argued that rearmament was essential for German security (because it was the price for a continued American commitment to Europe), for the integration of the FRG into the European and Atlantic communities as a respected equal (because the remaining occupation controls would be terminated), and for reunification itself (because an Allied position of strength in Western Europe was the prerequisite for fruitful negotiations with the Soviet Union). The FRG was admitted into the furbished-up Brussels pact and NATO in May 1955.

The Soviet government used diplomacy, including various proposals for a reunified and neutral Germany, to try to block the formation of a German army, but both the American and the Adenauer governments considered the FRG's rearmament and alliance with the West as nonnegotiable, neutralization on any terms as unacceptable. In September 1955 the Russians and West Germans agreed to establish diplomatic relations—a clear signal of the acceptance of a two-Germanys policy by both. The open creation in early 1956 of an East German army made little international stir.

Between them, the superpowers completed and fixed the new system of state relations in Europe. There was no peace treaty. There were not even serious negotiations between the Russians and Americans. The very tension that blocked a formal peace settlement led to a solution of the problem of German power in Europe that would have been inconceivable in 1945.

Would a system that had not been made rigid by dividing Germany into two states and arming each as part of a preexisting military-political bloc have proved as stable as the system thus created? It is not easy to make a convincing case that some other outcome *which could have been achieved* would have been more stable or even would have served the interests of those states better. This judgment does not overlook the most conspicuous victims of European stability in this form, the nations of Eastern Europe. It does not exalt stability as a value over self-determination. But analytically it is true that the European system came to be what it is because it divided least those with power to affect it.

8
Challenges: East and West

In Europe since 1955 there have been many changes but little change. There is still a bipolar state system dominated by two superpowers vastly stronger than their allies; still asymmetry between the Western and Eastern subsystems; still a divided Germany, the larger part anchored to the West by choice, the smaller tied to the East by coercion.

Many developments since 1955 in their time seemed likely to bring about major changes in the system. Yet all have had remarkably little net effect on the system except to maintain it. The set of challenges examined in this chapter concerns the two problems which the system dealt with as it came into being: American-Soviet relations and Germany. These three states had the most power to change the system—and did not.

The Superpowers: Tension and Security

During one period, between 1958 and 1962, a series of crises raised fear of war. But there was no war. It may be that the Soviet government was determined never to let the challenges to the status quo that it stirred reach the point of seriously risking conflict. Or we may postulate that war has been averted because Western power has at all times succeeded in deterring Soviet aggression. In that case we must credit Soviet policy-makers with cautious behavior in face of a deterrent which the Western governments themselves over the years constantly—and publicly—undervalued.

At the same time, the United States and its allies were also effectively deterred. For all the talk during the Eisenhower Administration of "rollback" and "liberation," the West did not try to liberate Hungary in 1956 because the United States—for neither the first nor the last time—would not risk war with the Soviet Union to change the status quo in Europe. It seems clear, therefore, that the balance of power between East and West in Europe has remained remarkably unchanged as measured by its applicable political effectiveness despite far-reaching changes in doctrine and weaponry on both sides since 1955.

A persistent thread of commentary over the last decades has pointed to an eventual loosening of the Soviet grip on Eastern Europe. There has, of course, been a loosening of the Eastern bloc since Stalin's time. But successive Soviet leaders have shown no intention of allowing the countries of Eastern Europe to slip into the orbit of the United States, or of a French-led or German-led "European Europe." The Soviet government appears to have acted on the belief that it could preserve little influence in most of these countries should they recover policy independence.

But the Soviets have paid a price for this enforced control. Their position in Eastern Europe has necessarily deprived their diplomacy of the flexibility which might have allowed them to pursue with greater success their goal of weakening or breaking up the Western bloc. Especially serious for the Soviet Union was the immobilization of its policy in face of the fact that the West Germans *might* have been tempted to rethink their position in the Western alliance if they could ever have found reason to believe that the GDR position in the Eastern bloc might also be open for reconsideration. The Soviet leaders, one would have thought, had serious reasons to consider such a policy. But the Eastern bloc has proved too rigid to be tampered with, even by the Soviets who created it, and this has helped the Western bloc maintain itself in place. Soviet diplomacy has thus been able to accomplish no more than to obtain Western recognition of the Eastern status quo.

Although the Western countries have acquiesced in and recognized Soviet control in Eastern Europe they have never lost their sense of anxiety at the proximity of Soviet power which that control brought with it. This fact goes far toward accounting for the persistence of the Western subsystem alongside the Eastern. Yet Western unity, and the American commitment to the system, have been challenged more than once by a relaxation of tension.

At the Geneva summit of July 1955 Stalin's successors promoted the notion (dating from the 1920s) of peaceful coexistence. Geneva was an important moment in postwar relations. Both superpowers, armed with thermonuclear weapons and recognizing the need to minimize the risks of war between them, were coming to understand that they might have certain interests in common, and that it might be worthwhile to search for ways to expand this area of commonality. But this first essay in détente had no significant effect on the European system.

A period of acute tension that began in 1958 with the second Berlin crisis ended abruptly in 1962 when the Russians overreached themselves by placing missiles in Cuba, an act so rash as to suggest that they were after a global bargain of some kind with the United States, or at least something more comprehensive than a favorable settlement of the Berlin or German problems. Fear of war diminished sharply in Europe after the Cuban missile crisis of 1962 and has never returned to the level reached then. Partly as a result, the centrifugal forces that surfaced within the two blocs as tension between them diminished seemed to foreshadow a new order of things in Europe.

But the signs of basic change that had risen up so bravely soon lamely flickered out. The Prague spring ended in August 1968 in the invasion of Czechoslovakia by the Warsaw Pact nations, which reminded those who needed the lesson that Soviet hegemony over Eastern Europe was not about to wither away, nor the postwar European system with it. Even before as well as after that event, the West European governments (except, in a sense, for the French) never acted as if they held the view imputed to them by many American commentators that there was no longer

7
Consolidation of the Two-Bloc System: The German Problem

During the war all the allies considered what they should do after the victory to prevent renewed German aggression. The answer obviously lay in doing what was not done in 1919: somehow depriving the Germans of either the means or the will to commit aggression. One obvious device all of them played with was the idea of partitioning Germany, an idea on which the Big Three governments seemed agreed in principle in the autumn of 1943. But by the time of the Yalta meeting the American and particularly the British governments had second thoughts, and when the war ended none of the Big Three was still thinking seriously of partition.

But while they had turned aside from it as a policy goal, they had begun to implement it in the arrangements they made before the war ended for occupying defeated Germany. No one saw those arrangements as foreshadowing a partition of Germany on zonal lines. They were worked out as a practical framework for implementing common occupation policies during the interim period between the defeat and a peace treaty.

At Potsdam—from which France was excluded—the Big Three had little difficulty agreeing on a program to demilitarize and denazify Germany. They also managed to agree in principle to organize the machinery for devising a common economic policy for the four zones. In two major respects, however, their disagreements proved more important than their agreements.

Occupied Germany Divided

First, the Soviet Union made known that it had assigned to Polish administration the part of German territory in its zone up to the Oder and western Neisse rivers, which was thus subtracted from the area controlled by the four powers. The Western powers complained about this unilateral Soviet action, but in the end they acquiesced in it as part of a deal that also concerned reparations policy, while pretending to treat the line as only provisional.

Second, and even more significant, the Big Three could not reach agreement on a unified policy of drawing reparations from Germany. The Russians wanted all they could get from all zones. But by July 1945 the Americans and British were unwilling either to let the standard of living in their zones be reduced to what they considered a dangerous level or to maintain it by providing aid to replace material shipped as reparations to the U.S.S.R. This specific issue was meshed with a broader view that Germany should be deprived of its war-making potential but should remain an important industrial power, both because this was essential to the economic recovery of Europe as a whole and because a prosperous Germany was most likely eventually to become democratic and peaceful.

The outcome of Potsdam was to leave the total reparations bill undecided and to allow each occupying power to remove capital assets from its own zone, subject to later understandings as to overall production levels and economic policy for Germany as a whole. The Soviet Union was given limited access to the industrial wealth of the Ruhr. But the French refused to concur in setting up an economic administration for all four zones unless the Rhineland and the Ruhr were removed from the area that was to be included under the proposed central administration.

The Americans and the British acquiesced in the French veto, and cold war competition then killed whatever chance there may still have been in late 1945 for development away from partition.

The question of what might have happened had the central economic administration envisaged at Potsdam been set up during 1945 or 1946, or if the Big Three had at least set up such a system in their own zones, is perhaps the most fascinating might-have-been of postwar European history. Some have thought a single German government might have evolved and that a united—albeit probably neutralized—German state would eventually have emerged. Yet we can wonder whether either the Soviet Union or the Western powers would have risked letting their zones be swallowed up in a German state which would have been large, rich, and open because of neutralization to the influence of the other side. It is more likely that the central administration would have been swept away by the forces that did, in fact, lead to Germany's division.

What would have become of a united but neutralized Germany? Both advocates and critics of the Western policies that led to the establishment of a West German state assumed that the German people would never accept a divided Germany and that German irredentism would be a threat to peace. The former proclaimed that the Federal Republic of Germany would be only a temporary way station on the road to a Germany reunited "in freedom." The latter feared that the temporary would become permanent, but dangerously so.

But the temporary has lasted and defused the problem of German unity. There is no compelling reason to believe that establishing a three-zone administration in 1946 or a united and neutralized Germany later would have led to a more stable and peaceful Europe than the very stable and peaceful Europe that did in fact emerge. The momentum of the cold war blocked *both* the absorption of all of Germany into either of the two emerging blocs *and* development toward unity in neutrality after 1945. Thanks, ironically, to the cold war, the outcome of World War II was more sound, more lasting, and systemically more beneficent than that of World War I.

West Germany Emerges

With the emphasis in Western Europe on economic recovery following the initiation of the Marshall Plan, it was obvious that West Germany would be called on to play a large part. It was not a long step to the conclusion that a reviving Germany with an important role in a reviving Western Europe could not remain forever under the direct military rule of the occupying powers. In May 1947 the Americans and British agreed to set up a bizone German Economic Council to be elected by the *land* (state) parliaments—in effect a German proto-government. In June the Russians established a coordinating economic commission among the five *länder* of their zone. One year later the three Western powers, with the Benelux countries, announced their decision to establish a federal West German state and implemented a currency reform in their zones as a spur to economic revival.

The Soviet response was to blockade West Berlin, ostensibly because the Western powers had introduced the new currency there, but more probably to block the formation of the West German state by discouraging the Germans, if not the three allies, from proceeding. But the Western powers decided, almost reflexively, to hang on to their position in Berlin. The willingness of the West German politicians to go ahead in these circumstances pointed clearly to the future international role of the West German state.

The Berlin crisis, which lasted for 11 months, until the Soviet Union called off the blockade, was the first episode of the cold war seriously to threaten hot war. As such, it powerfully strengthened public support in West Germany, Western Europe and the United States for the new alliance against the Soviet Union. There was no restoration of four-power control of Germany or Berlin. The Federal Republic of Germany (FRG) was launched in September 1949. One month later, the German Democratic Republic (GDR) went into business with a parallel devolution of partial authority by the Soviet Union to a German government in its zone of occupation. The Berlin crisis consummated the division of Germany.

When did the division of Germany in this form become inevitable or irreversible? Probably before, and certainly not this was not consistent with the FRG's unabated security dependence on the United States, nor could it be sustained in the circumstances of the 1960s.

The government of Ludwig Erhard thus undertook to improve West German relations generally with the countries of Eastern Europe. This policy was important as the first effort *of German origin* to break openings in the cold war wall across Europe.

Following the 1968 invasion of Czechoslovakia, the government of Willy Brandt faced the dilemma of either pursuing a bolder Eastern policy or writing off such a policy altogether, presumably for a return to a cold war rigidity. With the support or acquiescence of the allies, he chose the former. A complicated diplomatic process eventuated in an interlinked group of agreements which provided for West German acceptance of the territorial status quo in Eastern Europe, balanced by an agree-

Willy Brandt, chancellor of the Federal Republic of Germany from 1969 to 1974, greatly eased tensions in Central Europe through his *Ostpolitik* (Eastern policy).

Wide World Photos

ment among the Big Four (the postwar occupying powers) establishing a less tense modus vivendi in Berlin.

There was much talk in the early 1970s that these arrangements were only the beginning of a process which might lead to a loosening of the Eastern bloc, or of both blocs, and the political coming together in some way of the two German states. But there was no realistic prospect that any German government would even consider renouncing its Western security ties for a mere mirage of reunification, or that the Soviet Union would do anything to make such a mirage less unreal.

From 1949 on, West Germany's neighbors had reason to be concerned that sooner or later it would try to use its great economic strength to assert some kind of local hegemony. There was no compelling reason, after all, to believe that the new democratic polity would prove stronger than that of Weimar after World War I, and some reason to think that the partition of the country would generate nationalist reactions. These fears were not unreasonable, yet they have turned out to be baseless. One of the strongest and most overlooked factors making for the emergence and survival of the postwar European system has been its acceptance by the West Germans as being in their interest in both tension and détente and the steady adaptation of their policies to the exigencies of that choice.

The Federal Republic's initial postwar choice to pursue integration with the West was realistic in the short term because it led to the early end of occupation controls and the restoration of self-government; in the middle and longer terms because it provided for security; and at all times because it signified the Germans' understanding that a bid for reunification or hegemony would not only be unsuccessful but disastrous for the benefits they derived from the postwar European system.

9
Challenges: Within the West

From 1955 to the present the three states most able to shake the European system have not done so: the United States and the Federal Republic of Germany by choice, the Soviet Union for some combination of reasons reflecting conservatism toward Eastern Europe and prudence toward Western. Much that they did, however, or were thought likely to do, strengthened the widely held notion that the system was in permanent jeopardy. So did the tense stability of Eastern Europe. The barrage of challenges from within the subsystem has received even more attention but has had no more lasting impact. Still, these internal challenges have reflected significant changes in the relations among the members of that subsystem. It is useful, therefore, to examine each of them and consider why they produced so little structural change.

Security

Since the Euratlantic subsystem came into being there has been almost unquestioned agreement among the member governments on the continued relevance and validity of the U.S.

guarantee to Western Europe in treaty form, the strategic nuclear power which backed that guarantee, and (except for France) the integrated military force in Europe headed by an American and including substantial U.S. forces. Yet at no time has there been a thorough meeting of minds among the allies about how to deter war and defend Europe if war comes. At the most basic level, these disagreements reflect the great differences among the geographical and power positions of a very disparate set of allies. No alliance of unequals can be untroubled. The problem of diverse outlooks and interests among the allies has been compounded by the steady march of military technology over the years.

Several conclusions can be drawn from the problems relating to security in the alliance which may have relevance for the future if, as is likely, the alliance will continue to be troubled by questions of how best to meet the persisting Soviet threat which is its security *raison d'être*.

First, though the alliance has undergone a chronic and public internal debate on strategic doctrine and related issues, war has been deterred and security maintained. The Russians have shown themselves to be most prudent in probing the alliance's self-advertised military deficiencies.

Second, the European allies on the whole have acted as if they understood that the alliance must have been doing some things well enough, if not well. In no case have they (except for France) been inclined to make the financial and political efforts required to do other than continue to rely on the U.S. guarantee and acquiesce in its current doctrines whatever their ambiguities. This has been true above all for the West Germans.

Third, European dependence on the U.S. security guarantee was so deep-seated as to be proof against the alliance deficiencies which vexed the Americans so much, the irritations inevitably caused by the dependence itself, and even the French attempt to exploit these problems. No doctrine, after all, was likely to satisfy all the allies all the time. The allies have generally acted as if they understood that they had no viable alternative to going along with the U.S. guarantee. If the U.S. government had also understood this fact, it might have spared itself and the allies much anguish in pursuit of a consensus on strategic doctrine that could not and did not need to be achieved.

A related American mistake in the 1960s was to overrate European concern about the implications for their security of U.S.-Soviet strategic parity. Misreading of both French and German policy led not only to clumsy efforts to stop the French nuclear force and to reinforce the links inhibiting the independence of the British force, but also to an attempt to give the Germans a "finger on the trigger" of a mock multilateral nuclear force while blocking what was judged, wrongly, to be their inevitable desire to catch up with France and achieve nuclear autonomy. Since that misadventure, few on either side of the Atlantic have wanted to delve into the dark recesses of nuclear sharing.

The turbulent history of the last two decades and more shows a consistently good performance by the debated alliance system with respect to its basic security purposes. Each year that has passed has, in fact, strengthened the common belief that the alliance would continue to work. That may seem complacent, but it reflects a fact that has been of great psychological and political value in stabilizing the alliance, the Western subsystem of which it is a part, and the European state system as a whole.

Economics

It is useful to see the web of economic relationship developed in the Euratlantic subsystem as forming also an economic system in itself. The United States and the European states, which were the metropoles for colonial or postcolonial economic relations with most of the world outside the Soviet sphere of control, have been members of a truly global economic system, supplementing their extra-European political involvements. The trade and monetary systems of the non-Communist states of the world have been managed mainly by countries which were security and political allies in the Euratlantic subsystem, plus one other U.S. ally, Japan, which was readily co-opted into the existing system when its economic strength revived—a testimony to the ability of the system to adapt to new conditions.

What has been the balance sheet of the postwar economic

system up to the present? One touchstone for measuring any economic system is growth. On that score, the system has been an immense success for all its advanced members. There has been a marked increase in the standard of living of the large majority of their populations in the postwar period as a whole. This has clearly contributed a great deal to the stability of democratic constitutional arrangements in postwar Europe and has helped promote that acceptance of diminished status after decades of fevered nationalism which has characterized most European countries since the war.

The economic system has also helped knit the members together. The new wealth has been accompanied by the growing importance of foreign trade for all members. The preponderant share of that trade has been carried on among them. These patterns of trade have been reinforced by the increasing interpenetration of investment among these countries and their participation in an international monetary system based on the Bretton Woods machinery established at the end of World War II.

The Atlantic states began to face economic difficulties almost as soon as currency convertibility—and the European Economic Community (Common Market)—came into being, regarding such things as the "inward-looking" price support and tariff system the Community maintained for its agricultural produce. But it was in the interest of both the United States and the Community to prevent trade wars and to keep such issues in bounds. And, while selective protectionism has been maintained, they have done so.

There were much more serious difficulties besetting the Western economic system continuously from the late 1950s related to the monetary challenge, the third world challenge, and the challenge in the 1970s of inflation, unemployment, and the dislocation of prosperity. No sooner had the Bretton Woods monetary system come into full operation in 1958, with the establishment of convertibility among fixed-rate Western currencies, than the belief began to spread that the payments deficit which the United States had been running since 1950 could not continue indefinitely. But policy-makers came more and more to

Don Wright in *The Miami News,* 1971

The Nixon-Connally "shocks" of 1971 drew criticism at home as well as abroad.

the conclusion that the deeper problem which the deficits represented could not be resolved in the Bretton Woods system as it stood because, while they were a threat to long-term international monetary stability and economic growth, they were at the same time essential to financing world trade. The United States, having become a global "central bank," had reasons beyond domestic convenience or even hegemony not to dry up too quickly the main instrument for increasing world liquidity.

What the U.S. government proposed was that the IMF provide additional drawing rights to its members without additional payments—what became, after the Rio de Janeiro meeting in 1967, Special Drawing Rights. This was a signal step toward the transformation of the IMF into a global bank of emission and the emergence of a new currency to supplement, perhaps eventually largely replace, gold, dollars and pounds sterling in international transactions. But there was continuing reluctance in all governments, particularly those of reserve currency countries, to recognize that their international economic situations, and the international monetary system as a whole, were in a state of fundamental disequilibrium because they themselves were less and less willing to subject their economies to the measures required to maintain exchange rates.

In the end the essential step toward replacing, or at least demolishing, the Bretton Woods system was taken unilaterally by the United States. On August 15, 1971 the American government "temporarily" suspended the convertibility of dollars into gold, imposed a 10 percent surcharge on dutiable imports, and invoked a wage-price freeze. The form and substance of the American action produced the most severe crisis over economic issues that the United States and its major partners have ever experienced. It was, in fact, a major crisis of the Atlantic relationship, and of U.S.-Japanese relations as well. A relationship that survived that crisis had strong roots indeed.

With the Smithsonian Agreement of December 1971 the United States won an improvement in its trade position by the realignment of exchange rates, but the new rates proved as untenable as the old. Indeed, the quick return of monetary crisis demonstrated that a regime of fixed rates could not be maintained without stringent capital controls and rigorous manipulation of domestic economies, neither of which was tolerable to most countries. Yet one more sterling crisis, in June 1972, ended with the floating of the pound and a massive flight from the dollar. Yet another round of speculation, in February and March 1973, led to a second devaluation of the dollar and the addition of the Swiss franc, the yen, and the currencies of the European Community to the list of those floating. This, it has turned out, is the post-Bretton Woods monetary system. The temporary regime became not only tolerable but acceptable. There were two main reasons for this.

First, the floating of most major currencies, including the dollar, had been thought of initially as a provisional arrangement suitable to counter speculative movements until something more permanent could be devised. But in the inflation that prevailed after 1972, and the recession that accompanied it after 1974, managed floating was soon found to be a workable means of balance-of-payments adjustment, more symmetrical than the old system in placing some responsibility for adjustment on surplus as well as deficit countries and with fewer of the burdens of a fixed rate system which had come to seem unacceptable.

The second reason is that the quadrupling of the price of oil by the oil exporters in late 1973 radically changed the priorities of the advanced countries which until then had dominated discussions of a new monetary system. Those issues faded in importance compared to the urgent problems of finding ways to finance their oil purchases and counter the recessionary impact of the price increase. In short, the very breakdown of the Bretton Woods system and the efforts expended on trying to replace it or managing to live without a replacement imposed an unprecedented degree of practical cooperation among the leading countries.

The powerful eruption of the Organization of Petroleum Exporting Countries (OPEC) into the world's economic consciousness in late 1973 caused the main focus of international negotiation to shift from the monetary plane to what came to be called the North-South dialogue on problems of resource distribution. For the advanced countries the main issues were, first, how to finance their oil imports, and second, whether or how to concert their approach to the less-developed countries to maintain their economic strength in light of changed circumstances (higher energy costs) and the threat of further change (redistribution of the world's wealth to the relative benefit of the poor through what the less-developed countries came to call a New International Economic Order).

It was fortunate that the advanced countries were operating at this point on a regime of floating exchange rates, which made it easier for them to adapt without constant monetary crises to the potentially destabilizing fact that the burden of oil imports did not fall with equal effects on all of them. The United States, which imported much less of its energy needs than Japan and the countries of Western Europe, suddenly found itself in a far stronger economic position vis-à-vis them than had been the case for many years.

If the worst effects of the oil price rise that were foreseen did not take place, it is because the OPEC surplus countries have had to use their money somehow. The oil sellers have bought more goods and services from the West than had been expected; have invested some of their proceeds in the West; and have deposited their money with U.S. and European banks which, in turn, have lent it out or "recycled" it in such a way as to supply the means to all the advanced countries in deficit to pay their oil bills. This is clearly not a dependable, long-term arrangement. Even so, the international monetary system up to the present has managed the consequences of the oil price increases with less disruption of the Western economies—and Western political relations—than had been expected. Indeed, Western unity has to some extent been strengthened.

The main Western countries have tried to deal with their common economic problems by, among other means, a new consultative mechanism: the Western economic summit. Cooperation has succeeded once again in at least warding off policies that they might have been tempted to use in the circumstances and that would have had a negative impact on all of them. If the major advanced countries have all been baffled about how to restrain prices while reducing unemployment to politically and socially acceptable levels, they have at any rate been baffled together and have acted on the whole as if they understood that no one of them could solve its problems by itself.

Hanging Together and Hanging Separately

The degree of economic policy cooperation which the Western countries achieved had tended to be overlooked not only because of the real disagreements among them but also because of the institutional untidiness with which they conducted their economic relations. Far from working through a single institution, they made use of the IMF, the Organization for Economic Development, the General Agreement on Tariffs and Trade (GATT) and the UN, among others. The fact that Western economic policy was made by practically the same countries as determined Western security policy helps account for the fact that the policies of these countries on the economic plane on the whole reinforced and were reinforced by their association in other ways. Yet there is a seeming paradox to be explained in the fact that none of the main instruments of economic cooperation was connected with the Atlantic alliance.

One obvious reason is that Japan and a few other advanced countries were not members of the alliance. A second reason is that some of the allies probably did not want to make even more explicit the tie which they were well aware existed among security, political, and economic problems and to make even stronger the advantage this tie gave the United States, dominant in the first field and in the alliance, with respect to American dealings with them on other matters. A third reason was simply that several other useful organizations were already operating when the alliance came along. GATT, the IMF, and the rest provided forums in which non-Atlantic countries could take part on a nondiscriminatory basis.

The notion has been widespread that the alliance had to take on new functions and new missions if it was not to lose public confidence in its ability to handle the old. But efforts to widen the alliance's scope into economic problems have largely failed. In this case, as in so many others, the alliance was not seriously harmed even by overambitious and unnecessary efforts to improve it—another sign of its basic good health.

The difficulty which the alliance has experienced in trying to expand its scope into economic and also extra-European matters is nicely counterpointed by the relative ease with which it *has* developed a most important "second leg," the coordination of members' policies with respect to détente. There was widespread concern beginning in the late 1960s not only that "détente fever" would corrode NATO's defense base but that there would be a competitive "rush to Moscow" by the allies that would be detrimental to the security of all of them. Yet that did not happen.

The record of the last ten years is not without suspicions and divisions among the allies, but on the whole it shows that the alliance adapted itself very effectively to the technical needs of multilateral diplomacy and to the political needs of pursuing détente in a way that was consistent with continued defense requirements and with alliance cohesion. The allies had little choice but to succeed.

This discussion suggests that the much-debated question of how to make the Atlantic alliance into a community has been sterile. The alliance has not had to develop into anything beyond itself to survive and, by any realistic measure, to prosper. Both the United States and its European allies have felt that their ultimate security and well-being were more bound up with each other than with any others. Unless the word community is a code for federal state (in which case the goal is nonsense) or unless structural tidiness is a required element in a community, it is entirely proper to say that an Atlantic community is already in existence and has long been. It is, in fact, the Euratlantic subsystem which has been under discussion throughout this book.

The Uniting of Europe

It may seem surprising for the concept of European unity to be described as a challenge to the postwar European system. Yet it is not so surprising if we remember that the word challenge is used in this book to describe any development with the potential to make a major structural change in the essentially bipolar system dominated by the two superpowers. It is obvious that a united Western Europe would have a profound impact on that system.

Jean Monnet, a political economist and diplomat who never held elective office, was the driving intellectual force behind the idea of the European Economic Community.

Wide World Photos

Whether such a Europe became a more or less equal ally of the United States or something closer to a third force between the superpowers, the resulting state system would have been very different from that with which we are familiar.

Before it became clear that Western Europe would be caught up in a half-continental system led by the United States and that, in any case, there was no possibility in the cold war for a revival of intra-European conflict, the idea of a united Europe presented itself as the logical way to avoid repeating the bloody divisions of the past, as well as to enhance Europe's sadly diminished status. After the bold proposal made by French Foreign Minister Robert Schuman in 1950 to place the French and West German coal and steel industries under a joint authority with supranational powers, the policy of moving progressively toward greater Western European unity by means of delegating specific functional powers to a supranational authority rapidly became a cause.

By two treaties signed at Rome in March 1957, the Six (France, the FRG, Italy, and the Benelux countries) established the European Economic Community (EEC) and the European Atomic Energy Community (Euratom). General de Gaulle opposed the treaties, but when he returned to power in 1958 he decided to accept them as the framework for his own policy of creating a French-led bloc in Western Europe. The Community survived de Gaulle but it has never returned to the path from which he diverted it. For all we know, less than unanimous decision-making and other possible developments which he blocked might have enabled it to grow slowly into a federal-like system.

But other, more basic considerations suggest that the Community would not have marched forward inevitably to federal union even without de Gaulle. Common economic policy, for one, has proved impossible to achieve. National economies were usually somewhat out of phase with each other at any given time and national attitudes toward the priorities of economic policy traditionally differed.

The members of the Community have been even less successful in developing a coordinated and autonomous foreign policy, and least successful in the realm of defense arrangements. The European allies have had their problems with NATO but never to the point that they were impelled to organize a European defense effort either to increase their influence within the alliance or to replace it. This would have presupposed a political unity which they never achieved and cost and effort which it is difficult to imagine their accepting. Even then one can ask whether Western Europe could ever have a credible defense strategy *of its own* whatever armament effort was made.

Since the degree of integration achieved by the EEC did not automatically engender an even greater degree, the only real alternative to the ambiguous outcome we have seen would have been for the Europeans to have delegated substantial further powers to a central authority—that is, to have established a federal state to conduct foreign and defense policy. But this they have not been willing to do.

Whatever the causes for the waning of the European impulse, the fact is plain and the implications to date seem obvious. As the Germans turned aside from the dream of reunification to pursue more attainable goals, so the Europeans have seemed satisfied to use the Community machinery for their common good, but to do so, and to pursue their other interests, in the Atlantic framework. Many have deplored and condemned this alleged European loss of will and purpose. But more has been lost than political greatness and global reach. The art critic John Russell has written:

> What was lost to Europe between 1900 and 1950, and above all between 1939 and 1945, was the sense of predestined leadership which had been taken for granted since the days of Plato and Virgil, Charlemagne and the builders of Chartres Cathedral.

My own conclusion is that the Europeans have adapted with much intelligence to the postwar world in which they found themselves. The conflict between adaptation to a sadly imperfect world and pursuit of possibly nobler but elusive goals has always been a staple of Western literature. Our hearts go out to the heroes of quest but our heads, on reflection, may sometimes give the palm to their brothers who learn how to survive.

Charles de Gaulle, president of France, 1958–69 and founder of the Fifth Republic.

Wide World Photos

The French Challenge

A common thread running through the history of the movement for European union was the effort of French governments to use the Europe of Six as the vehicle for asserting their own leadership in Europe and France's status in the world. This goal underlay all French foreign policy since the war.

From the start France was the most reluctant member of the Euratlantic system as it stood. It tried to magnify its voice in Europe by clinging at great cost to colonial possessions which it could not hold. The climax of this rearguard action was the Suez debacle in 1956, its finale was the stubborn escalation of the effort to repress the Algerian revolution.

De Gaulle worked to remove all serious limitation on France's freedom of action in international affairs. Above all, he reversed the integration of France in Atlantic and European organizations which might deprive it of its ability to make decisions based on its own interests. He tried at first to win recognition of France's status by means of the 1958 proposal for a tripartite directorate to manage the cold war globally. When the Americans refused this direct proposal, de Gaulle then set about coercing them into accepting his demand. He predictably dis-integrated France from NATO's military system (while emphasizing continued loyalty to the North Atlantic Treaty and to the alliance) when it became clear that neither persuasion nor coercion would lead the United States to give France the status he wanted.

After 1963 he shifted from a rigid to a more open approach to the Soviet Union, obviously with the hope of using the Soviet Union as a lever to help him develop a French-led European bloc. He wanted to encourage the Europeans placed between the two colossi to take initiatives themselves. But his dream of a gradual loosening of both the Western and Eastern blocs was shattered by the demonstration of Soviet determination to maintain Russian control over Eastern Europe with the invasion of Czechoslovakia in 1968.

De Gaulle's hope to establish a confederal political community of the Six came to nothing because the other five strongly resented his brutal rejection of integration even in principle, and because they saw in his plan a desire to establish a European grouping under French leadership which would distance itself from the United States. But he clearly bears some—though not all—of the responsibility for weakening the European spirit and preventing further institutional evolution thereafter. By doing that, he perhaps blocked the growth of what would have been a more serious challenge than the one he himself mounted to the structure of the Euratlantic subsystems and the U.S. leadership of it which he so much deplored.

Economic problems and the diminution of prospects for an active détente policy have left France little latitude or opportunity for trying to organize and lead Europe or differentiate it from the United States. France under Valéry Giscard d'Estaing has pursued independent policies in pursuit of its interests. But they have not been designed to pose a significant challenge to the Euratlantic system, nor have they done so.

10
Toward the Future

The European state system developed by the cold war and completed by the arming of Germany in 1955 remains intact today. It will continue to be challenged by developments in the years to come, as it has been in the past. These challenges will have to contend against the hard factors which have maintained the structural stability of the European state system against the many serious challenges of the last quarter-century.

The Soviet Union is likely to maintain its strategic and political dominance over Eastern Europe. Its overwhelming power presence there and in Central Europe will continue to be seen by most Western Europeans as a threat to their security. The Western Europeans are likely to want to maintain a visible and structured alliance with the United States—in fact, the Atlantic alliance we have—to provide them with security. The United States, for its part, will almost certainly continue to play its established role in the Euratlantic subsystem.

The ties of alliance will be reinforced by common interests of other kinds, not least by the understanding of the member states that they have no real alternative to maintaining an effective and cooperative economic system among them.

U.S. Department of State

The superpower balance: Europe's two most important heads of state met in Vienna in June 1979.

The solution to the German problem which has been brought about by Soviet policy in Eastern Europe and by the Western European and American response to that is by now, and will probably remain, generally acceptable or at least tolerable to most Europeans, East and West, and even to the West Germans, *as compared to feasible alternatives.*

These premises may be eroded or bypassed by new challenges. But they are weighty elements of the situation. The factors of stability will not be lightly swept away. The state system which up to now has so well reflected the true balance of power in the Europe that has emerged from the crises of the 20th century has a strong lease on the future.

Talking It Over

A Note for Students and Discussion Groups

This pamphlet, like its predecessors in the HEADLINE Series, is published for every serious reader, specialized or not, who takes an interest in the subject. Many of our readers will be in classrooms, seminars or community discussion groups. Particularly with them in mind, we present below some discussion questions—suggested as a starting point only—and references for further reading.

Discussion Questions

In the first chapter the author outlines the long decline of the modern European system of states. What factors kept the system going for several centuries? What caused its breakdown in the 20th century?

Why does the author describe Europe between 1919 and 1939 as living in an "Indian summer"? Was the revival of German power inevitable? Why or why not? Was World War II inevitable? Why or why not?

Chapter 3 describes how World War II ended with the division of Europe between the new superpowers. Why was this the outcome of the war? Was some other outcome possible?

In chapter 4 the author outlines the policies which the United States and the Soviet Union brought into the postwar period. Comparing the two lists, do you think that conflict between them was inevitable? If not, what kind of agreements or compromises might they have worked out that could have satisfied the interests of both as outlined here?

What problems led to the breakdown of the wartime alliance into the cold war? What would one or both of the superpowers have had to do to avoid the cold war?

Why does the author say that the German problem was resolved as a by-product of cold war competition? Might it have been resolved in some other way? With what consequences for Europe and the relations between the superpowers?

The last two chapters review the many challenges which the new European system has faced in the last 25 years. Which were the most important? Which seemed at the time most likely to make an important difference in the postwar system? Why, in the author's view, did none basically change the system?

The author suggests that the system he describes in Europe is likely to endure for the foreseeable future. Why does he think so? What is your own judgment about this after reading this study?

READING REFERENCES

Cleveland, Harold van B., *The Atlantic Idea and Its European Rivals*. New York, McGraw-Hill, 1966.

Davis, Lynn Etheridge, *The Cold War Begins: Soviet-American Conflict Over Eastern Europe*. Princeton, N.J., Princeton University Press, 1974.

Gaddis, John Lewis, *The United States and the Origins of the Cold War, 1941-1947*. New York, Columbia University Press, 1972.

Gardner, Richard N., *Sterling-Dollar Diplomacy*. New York, McGraw-Hill, 1969.

Halle, Louis J., *The Cold War as History*. New York, Harper & Row, 1967.

Holborn, Hajo, *A History of Modern Germany, 1840-1945*. New York, Knopf, 1969.

Kolodziej, Edward A., *French International Policy Under de Gaulle and Pompidou: The Politics of Grandeur.* Ithaca, N.Y., Cornell University Press, 1974.

Landes, David S., ed., *Western Europe: The Trials of Partnership.* Lexington, Mass., Lexington Books, 1977.

Shonfield, Andrew, ed., *International Economic Relations of the Western World, 1959-1971,* 2 vols. New York, Oxford University Press, 1976.

Solomon, Robert, *The International Monetary System, 1945-1976.* New York, Harper & Row, 1977.

Taylor, A. J. P., *The Struggle For Mastery in Europe, 1848-1918.* London, Oxford University Press, 1954.

Ulam, Adam B., *Expansion and Coexistence: The History of Soviet Foreign Policy, 1917-1967.* New York, Praeger, 1968.

Willis, F. Roy, *France, Germany, and the New Europe, 1945-1967.* Stanford, Calif., Stanford University Press, 1968.

Wilson, Theodore A., "The Marshall Plan, 1947-51." HEADLINE Series 236. New York, Foreign Policy Association, June 1977.

Wolfe, Thomas W., *Soviet Power and Europe, 1945-70.* Baltimore and London, The Johns Hopkins Press, 1970.

Yergin, Daniel, *Shattered Peace: The Origins of the Cold War and the National Security State.* Boston, Houghton Mifflin, 1977.

Statement of Ownership, Management and Circulation

(Required by 39 U.S.C. 3685)

1. Title of publication: HEADLINE Series. 1a. Publication No: 238340.
2. Date of filing: September 28, 1979.
3. Frequency of issue: 5 times each year—Feb., Apr., August, Oct., Dec.
3a. No. of issues published annually: 5.
3b. Annual subscription price: $7.00.
4. Location of known office of publication: 205 Lexington Ave., New York, N.Y. 10016.
5. Location of the headquarters or general business offices of the publishers: Same.

6. Names and complete addresses of publisher, editor, and managing editor: Publisher—Foreign Policy Association, 205 Lexington Ave., New York, N.Y. 10016; Editor—Wallace Irwin, Jr., 205 Lexington Ave., New York, N.Y. 10016; Managing Editor—Nancy Hoepli, 205 Lexington Ave., New York, N.Y. 10016.

7. Owner: (If owned by a corporation, its name and address must be stated and also immediately thereunder the names and addresses of stockholders owning or holding 1 percent or more of total amount of stock. If not owned by a corporation, the names and addresses of the individual owners must be given. If owned by a partnership or other unincorporated firm, its name and address, as well as that of each individual must be given. If the publication is published by a nonprofit organization, its name and address must be stated.) Foreign Policy Association, Inc., 205 Lexington Ave., New York, N.Y. 10016.

8. Known bondholders, mortgagees, and other security holders owning or holding 1 percent or more of total amount of bonds, mortgages or other securities: (If there are none, so state) none.

9. For Completion by Nonprofit Organizations Authorized to Mail at Special Rates (Section 132.122, PSM): The purpose, function, and nonprofit status of this organization and the exempt status for Federal income tax purposes have not changed during preceding 12 months.

10.	Extent and Nature of Circulation	Average No. Copies Each Issue During Preceding 12 Months	Actual Number of Copies of Single Issue Published Nearest to Filing Date
A.	Total no. copies printed (Net Press Run)	13,674 incl. reprints	12,733
B.	Paid Circulation		
	1. Sales through dealers and carriers, street vendors and counter sales	3,371	384
	2. Mail subscriptions.	7,539	7,159
C.	Total paid circulation (Sum of 10B1 and 10B2)	10,910	7,543
D.	Free distribution by mail, carrier or other means Samples, complimentary, and other free copies	1,350	270
E.	Total distribution (Sum of C and D)	12,260	7,813
F.	Copies not distributed		
	1. Office use, left over, unaccounted, spoiled after printing	1,414	4,920
	2. Returns from news agents	none	none
G.	Total (Sum of E, F1 and 2—should equal net press run shown in A)	13,674	12,733

I certify that the statements made by me above are correct and complete.

DON DENNIS,
Business Manager